Vibration Analysis with SOLIDWORKS Simulation 2016

Paul M. Kurowski, Ph.D., P.Eng.

SDC
Publications

Design Generator, Inc.

SDC Publications
P.O. Box 1334
Mission, KS 66222
913-262-2664
www.SDCpublications.com
Publisher: Stephen Schroff

Examination Copies
Books received as examination copies are for review purposes only and may not be made available for student use. Resale of examination copies is prohibited.

Electronic Files
Any electronic files associated with this book are licensed to the original user only. These files may not be transferred to any other party.

Trademarks

SOLIDWORKS® is a registered trademark of Dassault Systémes SOLIDWORKS Corporation.

Microsoft Windows® and its family products are registered trademarks of the Microsoft Corporation.

Every effort has been made to provide an accurate text. The author and the manufacturers shall not be held liable for any parts or products developed with this book or held responsible for any inaccuracies or errors that appear in the book.

About the Cover

The image on the cover shows the sixth mode of vibration of FRAME model which can be found in Chapter 17: Response Spectrum Analysis. The sixth mode is for illustration only; it is not used in the analysis. All models used in this book may be downloaded from www.SDCPublications.com.

ISBN-13: 978-1-63057-012-5
ISBN-10: 1-63057-012-5

Printed and bound in the United States of America.

About the Author

Dr. Paul Kurowski obtained his MSc and PhD in Applied Mechanics from Warsaw Technical University. He completed postdoctoral work at Kyoto University. Dr. Kurowski is an Assistant Professor in the Department of Mechanical and Materials Engineering, at Western University. His teaching includes Finite Element Analysis, Product Design, Kinematics and Dynamics of Machines and Mechanical Vibrations. His interests focus on Computer Aided Engineering methods used as tools of product design.

Dr. Kurowski is also the President of Design Generator Inc., a consulting firm with expertise in Product Development, Design Analysis, and training in Computer Aided Engineering.

Dr. Kurowski has published many technical papers and taught professional development seminars for the SAE International, the American Society of Mechanical Engineers (ASME), the Association of Professional Engineers of Ontario (PEO), the Parametric Technology Corporation (PTC), Rand Worldwide, SOLIDWORKS Corporation and others.

Dr. Kurowski is a member of the Association of Professional Engineers of Ontario and the SAE International. He can be contacted at www.designgenerator.com

Acknowledgements

I would like to thank the students attending my various courses for their valuable comments and questions. I thank my wife Elżbieta for editing and proofreading the text and support that made it possible to write this book.

Paul Kurowski

Table of contents

Class Files

To download the files that are required for this book, type the following in the address bar of your web browser:

SDCpublications.com/downloads/978-1-63057-012-5

Before you start

Notes on hands-on exercises and functionality of Simulation

This book goes beyond a standard software manual. It takes a unique approach by bridging the theory of mechanical vibrations with examples showing the practical implementation of vibration analysis. This book builds on material covered in "**Engineering Analysis with SOLIDWORKS Simulation.**"

We recommend that you study the exercises in the order presented in the book. As you go through the exercises, you will notice that explanations and steps described in detail in earlier exercises are not repeated in later chapters. Each subsequent exercise assumes familiarity with software functions discussed in previous exercises and builds on the skills, experience, and understanding gained from previously presented problems.

Exercises in this book require **SOLIDWORKS Simulation**. The **SOLIDWORKS Simulation** Product Matrix document is available at:

www.SOLIDWORKS.com/sw/docs/SOLIDWORKS-simulation-matrix.pdf

Information on the **SOLIDWORKS Simulation** Packages is available at:

www.SOLIDWORKS.com/sw/products/10169_ENU_HTML.htm

All exercises in this book use **SOLIDWORKS** models, which can be downloaded from www.SDCpublications.com. Most of these exercises do not contain any **Simulation** studies; you are expected to create all studies, results plots, and graphs yourself. Animations of selected results may be found using YouTube link in www.designgenerator.com

All problems presented here have been solved with **SOLIDWORKS Simulation Premium** running on Windows 7 Professional.

Working on exercises you may notice that your results may be slightly different from results presented in this book. This is because numerical results may differ slightly depending on the operating system and software service pack.

We encourage you to explore each exercise beyond its description by investigating other options, other menu choices, and other ways to present results. You will soon discover that the same simple logic applies to all functions in **SOLIDWORKS Simulation**, be it structural, vibration or thermal analysis.

This book is not intended to replace software manuals. The knowledge acquired by the reader will not strictly be software specific. The same concepts, tools and methods apply to any FEA software.

1

Prerequisites

"**Vibration Analysis with SOLIDWORKS Simulation**" is not an introductory text to **SOLIDWORKS Simulation**. Rather, it picks up Vibration Analysis from where it was left in the pre-requisite textbook "**Engineering Analysis with SOLIDWORKS.**" If you are new to **SOLIDWORKS Simulation** we recommend reading "**Engineering Analysis with SOLIDWORKS Simulation**" to gain essential familiarity with Finite Element Analysis. At the very least go through chapters 4, 6, 18, 19 of this pre-requisite textbook.

The following prerequisites are recommended:

- ❑ An understanding of Vibration Analysis
- ❑ An understanding of Structural Analysis
- ❑ An understanding of Solid Mechanics
- ❑ Familiarity with **SOLIDWORKS**
- ❑ Familiarity with **SOLIDWORKS Simulation** to the extent covered in "**Engineering Analysis with SOLIDWORKS**" or equivalent experience
- ❑ Familiarity with the Windows Operating System

Selected terminology

The mouse pointer plays a very important role in executing various commands and providing user feedback. The mouse pointer is used to execute commands, select geometry, and invoke pop-up menus. We use Windows terminology when referring to mouse-pointer actions.

Item	Description
Click	Self-explanatory
Double-click	Self-explanatory
Click-inside	Click the left mouse button. Wait a second, and then click the left mouse button inside the pop-up menu or text box. Use this technique to modify the names of folders and icons in **SOLIDWORKS Simulation** Manager.
Drag and drop	Use the mouse to point to an object. Press and hold the left mouse button down. Move the mouse pointer to a new location. Release the left mouse button.
Right-click	Click the right mouse button. A pop-up menu is displayed. Use the left mouse button to select a desired menu command.

All **SOLIDWORKS** file names appear in CAPITAL letters, even though the actual file names may use a combination of capital and small letters. Selected menu items and **SOLIDWORKS Simulation** commands appear in **bold**; **SOLIDWORKS** configurations, **SOLIDWORKS Simulation** folders, icon names and study names appear in *italics* except in captions and comments to illustrations. **SOLIDWORKS** and **Simulation** also appear in bold font. Bold font is also used to draw the reader's attention to a particular term.

1: Introduction to vibration analysis

Topics covered

- ❑ Differences between a mechanism and a structure
- ❑ Difference between dynamic analysis and vibration analysis
- ❑ Rigid body motion and degrees of freedom
- ❑ Kinematic pairs
- ❑ Discrete and distributed vibration systems
- ❑ Single degree of freedom and multi degree of freedom vibration systems
- ❑ Mode of vibration
- ❑ Rigid Body Mode
- ❑ Modal superposition method
- ❑ Direct integration method
- ❑ Vibration Analysis with SOLIDWORKS Simulation and SOLIDWORKS Motion
- ❑ Functionality of SOLIDWORKS Simulation and SOLIDWORKS Motion
- ❑ Terminology issues

Differences between a mechanism and a structure

A mechanism is not firmly supported and can move without having to deform; components of a mechanism can move as rigid bodies. On the contrary, any motion of a structure must involve deformation because a structure is, by definition, firmly supported. This motion may take the form of a one-time deformation when a static load is applied, or the structure may be oscillating about the position of equilibrium when a time varying load is present. In short, a mechanism may move without having to deform its components while any motion of a structure must be accompanied by deformation. If an object can't move without experiencing deformation then it can be classified as a structure. Examples of mechanism and structure are shown in Figure 1-1.

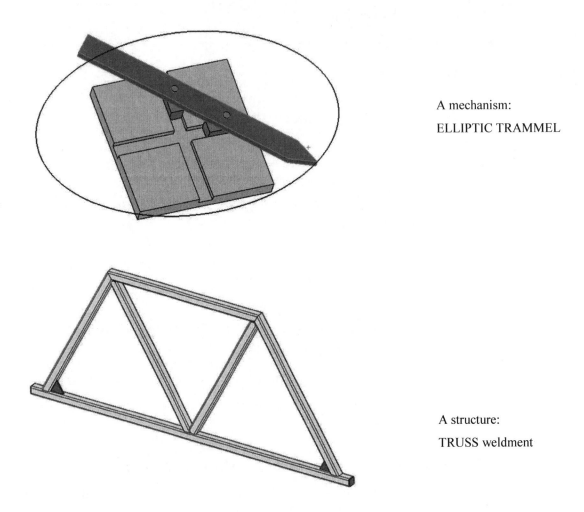

A mechanism:
ELLIPTIC TRAMMEL

A structure:
TRUSS weldment

Figure 1-1: A mechanism and a structure.

ELLIPTIC TRAMMEL model is discussed in this chapter; TRUSS model comes from "Engineering Analysis with SOLIDWORKS Simulation," chapter 16.

An elliptic trammel is a mechanism; it is designed to trace an ellipse when it performs motion. This motion can be studied without considering deformation of its components. A weldment is a structure. It is designed to stand still and can move only as it deforms from its position of equilibrium. Any motion of a structure is always accompanied by deformation.

Depending on the objective of analysis, an object or its components may be treated either as a mechanism or a structure. A wind turbine rotor is a mechanism; it spins relative to the tower. Depending on the objective of analysis this mechanism may be treated as a rigid body mechanism or an elastic body mechanism. An individual blade may be treated as a rigid body component of a mechanism or as a structure if its vibration characteristics need to be analyzed (Figure 1-2).

Figure 1-2: A helicopter rotor may be considered either as a mechanism consisting of deformable blades or of rigid blades.

Difference between Dynamic Analysis and Vibration Analysis

Dynamic Analysis can be performed on a mechanism or a structure. The analyzed object can be an airplane wing, a car, a building subjected to an earthquake, an engine or a door bell making sound. Dynamic Analysis can deal with rigid and/or elastic bodies. **Vibration Analysis** is more specific, it deals only with elastic bodies vibrating about the position of equilibrium.

Rigid body motion and degrees of freedom

If an object moves without deforming, then this object is called a **Rigid Body** and the motion is classified as a **Rigid Body Motion**. The number of independent variables necessary to define the position of a rigid body with respect to a reference coordinate system equals the number of degrees of freedom of that body. The number of degrees of freedom of a rigid body is equal to the number of rigid body motions of that body.

Consider an unsupported rigid body; to define its position with respect to a Cartesian coordinate system we need to provide six pieces of information: linear coordinates x, y, z along any point belonging to this body, and three angles defining angular orientation of the body (Figure 1-3).

Figure 1-3: A flying plane considered as a rigid body has six degrees of freedom or six rigid body modes.

Source of model: GrabCAD.

In the case of a flying airplane, three linear coordinates are required to define the position of the center of mass and three angular coordinates are required to define the angular position.

Kinematic Pairs

A kinematic pair is comprised of two rigid bodies; one rigid body is fully restrained, meaning it has no degrees of freedom. The other rigid body can move and is connected to the fully restrained body in such a way that the number of degrees of freedom of the moving body is limited.

We will review basic kinematic pairs and their Degrees of Freedom (DOF) using the assembly models listed in Figure 1-4. Notice that all assemblies are not fully defined to allow for relative motion of assembly components.

Kinematic pair	Number of translational DOF	Number of rotational DOF	SOLIDWORKS Assembly file name
Planar	2	1	PLANAR
Prismatic	1	0	PRISMATIC
Revolute	0	1	REVOLUTE
Cylindrical	1	1	CYLINDRICAL
Spherical	0	3	SPHERICAL
Screw	1/2	1/2	SCREW

Figure 1-4: A summary of basic kinematic pairs and their number of degrees of freedom.

If opened in SOLIDWORKS, you will find all assemblies consist of two components: the blue part is fixed (fully restrained) and the yellow part can move relative to the blue part.

To review the above models, use assembly commands **Move Component** and **Rotate Component**. No **SOLIDWORKS Simulation** study is required. In all examples featuring kinematic pairs, the fixed bodies are blue, and the moving bodies are yellow. Animation of the above kinematic pairs can be easily done in **SOLIDWORKS Motion**.

A **planar** kinematic pair is shown in Figure 1-5.

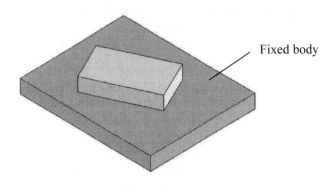

Fixed body

PLANAR.SLDASM

Figure 1-5: A planar kinematic pair removes three degrees of freedom from the moving body.

Two linear coordinates are required to define the position of the center of the sliding block and one angular coordinate is required to define its angular position. Therefore, the pair has two translational degrees of freedom and one rotational degree of freedom.

A **prismatic** kinematic pair is shown in Figure 1-6.

Fixed body

PRISMATIC.SLDASM

Figure 1-6: A prismatic kinematic pair removes five degrees of freedom from the moving body.

One linear coordinate is required to define the position of the sliding block. This pair has one translational degree of freedom.

A **revolute** kinematic pair is shown in **Figure** 1-7.

REVOLUTE.SLDASM

Figure 1-7: A revolute kinematic pair removes five degrees of freedom from the moving body.

One angular coordinate is required to define the position of the moving part. The pair has one rotational degree of freedom.

A **cylindrical** kinematic pair is shown in **Figure** 1-8.

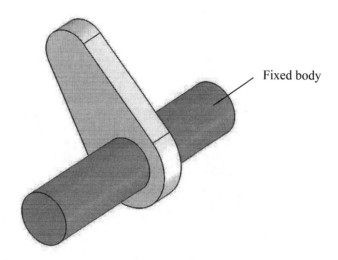

CYLINDRICAL.SLDASM

Figure 1-8: A cylindrical kinematic pair removes four degrees of freedom from the moving body.

One linear coordinate and one angular coordinate are required to define the position of the moving part. The pair has one translational and one rotational degree of freedom.

A **spherical** kinematic pair is shown in **Figure** 1-9.

SPHERICAL.SLDASM

Figure 1-9: A spherical kinematic pair removes three degrees of freedom from the moving body.

Three angular coordinates are required to define the position of the moving part. The pair has three rotational degrees of freedom.

A **screw** kinematic pair is shown in Figure 1-10.

SCREW.SLDASM

Figure 1-10: A screw kinematic pair removes five degrees of freedom from the moving body.

Either linear or angular coordinates fully define the position of the nut. The pair has one degree of freedom that couples translation and rotation. When you review this model, notice that the thread is not modeled explicitly. Instead, its presence is modeled by a mechanical mate. Cosmetic thread is added to the model appearance.

Discrete and distributed vibration systems

All that is required for vibration is a mass and stiffness. Therefore any real life object can be treated as a vibration system.

Depending on how mass and stiffness are distributed we can classify vibration systems as discrete or distributed systems. A discrete system is one where mass and stiffness are separated meaning that certain portions of the system are responsible for inertial properties while others are responsible for stiffness properties. Figure 1-11 shows two discrete systems: a single degree of freedom system and a two degree of freedom system. Both systems perform linear vibrations; the base and masses are treated as rigid bodies; deformations are limited to the springs which have no mass. Review the assembly model DISCRETE LINEAR in configurations *1DOF* and *2DOF* as shown in Figure 1-11.

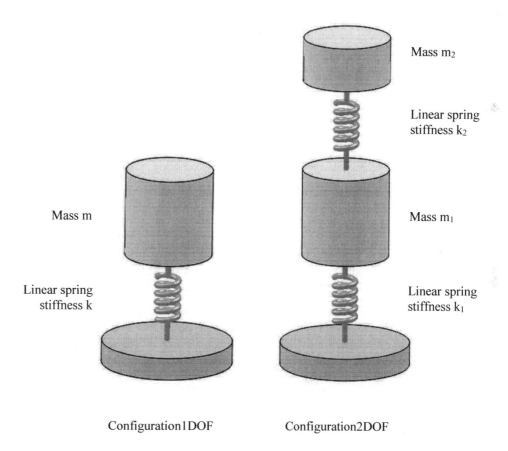

| Configuration1DOF | Configuration2DOF |

Figure 1-11: A single degree of freedom system (left) and two degree of freedom system (right) have mass and stiffness separated.

The cylindrical masses can move only in the vertical direction; they can't rotate. The base is fixed in both models.

One linear coordinate is required to define the position of the vibrating mass in the 1DOF model; two linear coordinates are required to define the positions of two vibrating masses in the 2DOF model.

A single degree of freedom (SDOF) discrete vibration system is a "workhorse" of the theory of vibration. Vibration responses of a SDOF have simple analytical solutions and many real life problems can be successfully studied by representing the system as an SDOF. We will study an SDOF in the second chapter to introduce essential concepts of vibration analysis with **SOLIDWORKS Simulation** and **SOLIDWORKS Motion**.

A discrete vibrating system can also perform rotary (angular) vibration. An example is the SWING ARM assembly model shown in Figure 1-12. The base and arm are treated as rigid bodies; deformation is limited to the massless spring.

Axis of rotation

Figure 1-12: A single degree of freedom rotary vibration system has mass and stiffness separated.

One angular coordinate is required to define the position of this system.

Referring to Figure 1-12, notice that the arm performs angular vibration, therefore vibration properties are defined by its mass moment of inertia about the axis of rotation. The spring experiences linear deformation; therefore, its vibration properties are defined by linear stiffness. The swing arm could also perform angular vibration if a torsional spring was installed at the hinge.

Discrete systems don't exist in real life and discrete representation is only a modeling simplification. We use discrete system representations because many problems can be described with sufficient accuracy by discrete models, usually with a few degrees of freedom. Degrees of freedom of discrete systems are clearly defined because deformation is limited to springs (linear and angular) present in the model. Analytical solutions of discrete systems are simple and results are often intuitive.

In a distributed vibrating system, mass and stiffness are not separated. All portions of an object are responsible for both mass and stiffness properties. Figure 1-13 shows the model CLIP which represents a distributed vibration system.

Figure 1-13: In a distributed vibration system, all portions of the object are responsible for both mass and stiffness properties.

Mass and stiffness are not separated.

Mode of vibration

The mode of vibration is the most fundamental property of any vibrating system. Its central role in vibration analysis requires us to discuss it in this introductory chapter. We will refine this definition later.

The mode of vibration can be defined as the preferred way of a structure to vibrate. It is characterized by its frequency of vibration, mass participating in the vibration, and shape of vibration. The number of modes of vibration is equal to the number of degrees of freedom of the vibrating system.

Shapes of vibration in the first (and only) mode of the discrete vibration system DISCRETE LINEAR in the *1DOF* configuration is shown in Figure 1-14. This model is available with **Frequency** studies set up and ready to run. Please run the solutions before proceeding.

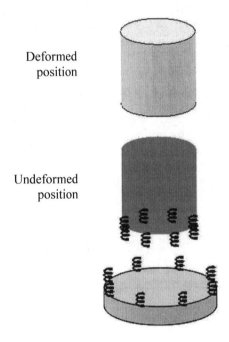

Deformed position

Undeformed position

Figure 1-14: The shape of vibration of the 1DOF model. The moving part translates as a rigid body; it does not experience any deformation. The only deforming element is the spring.

The mass moves as a rigid body; its motion is restricted to translation. Motion of the moving part is not restricted by any kinematic pair in this model. Distributed spring connector and restraints are defined in Frequency study: it is shown connecting components in the undeformed position.

Notice that the "Deformed shape" shown in Figure 1-14 refers to the deformation of the spring even though the spring deformation can't be seen on this illustration. The cylinder itself is not deforming; it performs linear oscillations as a rigid body.

The SWING ARM model in the *1DOF* configuration also has a **Frequency** study defined; please run the solution before proceeding.

Figure 1-15: Shape of vibration of the SWING ARM model.

The arm rotates as a rigid body; it does not experience any deformation. The only deforming element is the spring. Motion of the arm is controlled by a hinge.

Review assembly model SWING ARM and notice that the vertical post in the base serves only to locate the hinge position of the swing arm. The hinge itself is not modeled. The hinge is simulated in the **Frequency** study using a **Fixed Hinge** restraint.

A two degree of freedom discrete system has two modes of vibration, each one characterized by its own unique shape as demonstrated by the assembly model DOUBLE PENDULUM, shown in Figure 1-16. Run the **Frequency** study before proceeding.

Fixed link   Fixed link

Mode 1   Mode 2

Figure 1-16: Shapes of vibration of the DOUBLE PENDULUM model.

The shape of mode 1 and mode 2 are result plots in the Frequency study. The undeformed shape is superimposed on the deformed model.

Review the **Frequency** study in the DOUBLE PENDULUM model. Notice that **Global Contact** is set to **Allow Penetration** in order to disconnect the touching faces which otherwise would be bonded. The three links are connected by two **Pin Connectors** which have torsional stiffness and therefore act as torsional springs.

Distributed systems, where deformation is not limited to discrete springs, have an infinite number of degrees of freedom and consequently, an infinite number of modes of vibration. Consider CLIP (Figure 1-13) to be unsupported. CLIP treated as a rigid body has six degrees of freedom: three translations and three rotations; we may say it has six rigid body motions. When treated as an elastic body, CLIP will have an infinite number of degrees of freedom associated with elastic deformation in addition to those six degrees of freedom associated with **Rigid Body Motions (RBMs)**. Consequently it has an infinite number of modes of vibration. When this CLIP is analyzed using FEA, the number of elastic degrees of freedom becomes finite due to discretization which is an inherent part of FEA (Figure 1-17).

CAD model   Finite element mesh and mesh details

Figure 1-17: CLIP model before and after discretization.

Meshing was performed using second order tetrahedral solid elements with a default element size. This produced a mesh with 13326 nodes.

Remembering that solid elements have three degrees of freedom per node, the number of degrees of freedoms in the finite element mesh is 39978.

The total number of degrees of freedom is found by adding:

	Number of associated degrees of freedom
Rigid body motions	6
Deformation	39978
Total:	39984

The CLIP model after discretization has 39978 DOFs associated with deformation; most often this will be elastic deformation. Theoretically, this gives the model 39978 modes of vibration. However, all those higher modes are never excited in real life. Only the first few modes with frequencies low enough to be excited are important in the vibration response.

When the model is unsupported (as is the CLIP model) **Simulation** detects six **Rigid Body Modes** and assigns them frequencies of 0Hz. The first three modes are rigid body translations and the second three are rigid body rotations (Figure 1-18).

Translation along x

Translation along y

Translation along z

Rotation about x

Rotation about y

Rotation about z

Figure 1-18: Six Rigid Body Modes of the unsupported CLIP model are in this case aligned with the directions of the global coordinate system.

The dark shaded shape shows the undeformed model.

The directions of RBMs happen to be aligned with the global coordinate system in the CLIP model example, but this is not always the case.

Notice that the **Rigid Body Motion** and **Rigid Body Mode** terms may be considered interchangeable. In vibration theory, **Rigid Body Mode** is more frequently used.

Mode 7 and all higher modes are elastic modes of vibration. In most cases we don't count Rigid Body Modes (if they are present at all) and mode numbering starts from the first elastic mode. Figure 1-19 shows the first four elastic modes of vibration which we will simply call the modes of vibration. The frequencies of the first four modes are within the range of 0-2600Hz.

Mode 1
403Hz

Mode 2
971Hz

Mode 3
1561Hz

Mode 4
2595Hz

Figure 1-19: The first four modes of vibration of the unsupported CLIP model.

The undeformed model is superimposed on the deformed plots.

How many modes of vibration are of practical importance depends on the expected frequency range of the expected excitation. Most often, higher modes of vibration can't be excited and therefore have no importance in vibration analysis of mechanical systems (Figure 1-20).

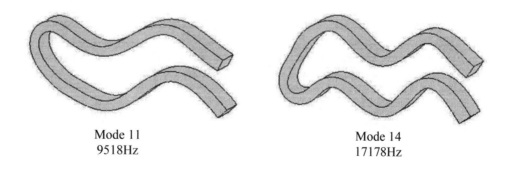

Mode 11
9518Hz

Mode 14
17178Hz

Figure 1-20: Higher modes have complex shapes and high frequencies.

The undeformed model is not shown.

Modal Superposition Method

The restrained and meshed with a default element size CLIP model has 39800 degrees of freedom. The exact number depends on how the restraints are defined. Solving this vibration problem would require finding a solution to the set of some 39800 equations. Considering that vibration problems are time dependent, those equations would have to be solved for all time steps where the number of time steps may be into the thousands. In the view of very high numerical effort required to solve vibration problems directly, we need a way to simplify the formulation of vibration problems. We will describe this process in steps.

Step 1

Let's summarize what we already know about modes of vibration. Each mode is characterized by frequency, shape of deformation, and the mass participating in the vibration. Furthermore, the direction of deformation is associated with certain stiffness. Collecting these facts we may represent an object vibrating in a given mode of vibration by a single degree of freedom oscillator with mass, stiffness and direction that correspond to the properties of the mode under consideration.

Step 2

Now we decide how many modes are important in the vibration response of the system under investigation. For example, if only three modes are important, we can represent the system with three Single Degree of Freedom oscillators (SDOF), each one corresponding to one mode. This way the number of degrees of freedom is reduced to just three, no matter how complex the model is.

Step 3

Instead of studying the original model, we may now study a simple 3DOF system where each mode is represented by a SDOF.

Step 4

We assume that the system is linear and we find its vibration response as a superposition of vibration responses of the three SDOFs.

The principle of the **Modal Superposition Method** is shown schematically in Figure 1-21.

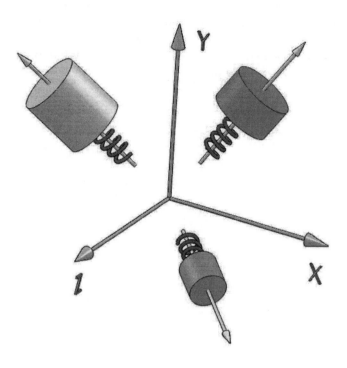

Figure 1-21: A vibration system represented by three single degree of freedom oscillators.

It is assumed that three modes of vibration are sufficient to model the vibration response. Each mode is represented by an SDOF oscillator. Each oscillator is characterized by its mass, stiffness and direction of linear displacement.

The **Modal Superposition Method** is universally used in vibration analysis with FEA. The most important condition that must be satisfied in order to use the **Modal Superposition Method** is that the problem must be **linear**. The second important issue is how many modes should be considered? This is most often decided by considering the frequency range of excitation. A convergence process may also be conducted where the same problem is solved a number of times, each time with more modes calculated to find the sensitivity of the data of interest to the number of modes considered in the **Modal Superposition Method**.

Direct Integration Method

An alternative to the **Modal Superposition Method** is the **Direct Integration Method**. It works with all degrees of freedom of the model. It does not require an assumption of the number of modes to be considered in a vibration response and the problem doesn't have to be linear. The **Direct Integration Method** is available in **SOLIDWORKS Simulation** but its numerical intensity limits practical applications to vibration problems of short time duration.

Vibration Analysis with SOLIDWORKS Motion and SOLIDWORKS Simulation

We have already defined discrete and distributed vibration systems; these definitions are essential to understanding differences between **SOLIDWORKS Simulation** and **SOLIDWORKS Motion** which are add-ins to **SOLIDWORKS**.

Vibration of discrete systems can be analyzed both by **SOLIDWORKS Motion** and **SOLIDWORKS Simulation**. Vibration of distributed systems can be analyzed only with SOLIDWORKS **Simulation.**

SOLIDWORKS Motion is a tool for kinematic and dynamic analyses of rigid bodies. Elasticity can be modeled in **SOLIDWORKS Motion** only as a discrete spring which makes it possible to use it for vibration analysis of discrete systems. Models analyzed by **SOLIDWORKS Motion** are typically mechanisms and have few degrees of freedom associated with rigid body motions of its components. All deformation is limited to springs. Vibration properties of distributed systems cannot be analyzed with **SOLIDWORKS Motion**.

SOLIDWORKS Simulation is a tool of structural analysis of elastic bodies by means of Finite Element Analysis. **SOLIDWORKS Simulation** models everything as elastic bodies with a large number of degrees of freedom and, consequently, with a large number of modes of vibration. It is up to the user to decide how many modes should be used to model a vibration response. Using **SOLIDWORKS Simulation**, a discrete representation of a problem does not offer any advantages besides a more intuitive understanding of the problem and the results. **SOLIDWORKS Simulation** performs discretization and represents every problem as a discrete system with a large but finite number of degrees of freedom.

Figure 1-22 shows the ELLIPTIC TRAMMEL model. This device can be used to trace an ellipse, hence the name. **SOLIDWORKS Motion** treats it as a mechanism. This mechanism has one degree of freedom and consists of two prismatic kinematic pairs and two revolute kinematic pairs. The angular position of the tracer or linear position of either slider fully defines the position of this mechanism. The elliptic trammel may become a vibration system if a torsional spring is added to either hinge. Then, any displacement will be associated with deformation, and the system will satisfy the requirements to be classified as a structure. Notice that the model with the torsional spring added still has one degree of freedom.

If the same model (with or without a spring) is analyzed with **SOLIDWORKS Simulation**, all components are treated as elastic bodies. The number of degrees of freedom will depend on the element size. If the default element size is used, the meshed model will have 14375 nodes and 43125 degrees of freedom.

Mesh Details	
Study name	Static 1 (-Default-)
Mesh type	Solid Mesh
Mesher Used	Standard mesh
Automatic Transition	Off
Include Mesh Auto Loops	Off
Jacobian points	4 points
Element size	4.8118 mm
Tolerance	0.24059 mm
Mesh quality	High
Total nodes	14346
Total elements	8312
Maximum Aspect Ratio	6.5693
Percentage of elements with Aspect Ratio < 3	98.8
Percentage of elements with Aspect Ratio > 10	0
% of distorted elements (Jacobian)	0
Remesh failed parts with incompatible mesh	Off
Time to complete mesh(hh:mm:ss)	00:00:01
Computer name	HPPAVILON

The model analyzed by **SOLIDWORKS Motion** has one degree of freedom; one piece of information fully defines the position of the mechanism.

The model analyzed by **SOLIDWORKS Simulation** has 14346 nodes; this translates into about 43000 degrees of freedom; the exact number depends on how restraints have been defined.

Figure 1-22: Different representations of the ELLIPTIC TRAMMEL model by SOLIDWORKS Motion (top) and SOLIDWORKS Simulation (bottom).

Animate the model in SOLIDWORKS motion to see that the tip of the arrowhead traces an ellipse.

SOLIDWORKS Motion works only with assemblies. Assembly components are modeled as solid bodies and are treated as undeformable (rigid bodies).

SOLIDWORKS Simulation works with both parts and assemblies and treats everything as elastic bodies.

Some problems analyzed with **SOLIDWORKS Motion** may give an appearance of analysis of deformable bodies but this is not what happens. Elastic properties must be added in contact definitions as is done in the WRECKING BALL model (Figure 1-23).

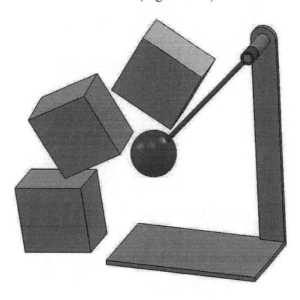

Figure 1-23: WRECKING BALL assembly analyzed with SOLIDWORKS Motion.

A stack of boxes is demolished by a wrecking ball.

As a result of the impact, boxes "fly apart" but deformation is not present anywhere in the model. Elastic properties of contact are assumed in SOLIDWORKS Motion. They must be entered by a user as a part of the model definition; alternatively, default values may be used.

Animation in **SOLIDWORKS Motion** may be completed using Animation, Basic Motion and Motion Analysis. Animations of ELLIPTIC TRAMMEL and WRECKING BALL have been set up using Motion Analysis; correct replays require Motion Analysis.

Capabilities of **SOLIDWORKS Simulation** and **SOLIDWORKS Motion** with regard to modeling discrete and distributed systems are summarized in Figure 1-24.

	Discrete systems	Distributed systems
SOLIDWORKS Simulation	Yes	Yes
SOLIDWORKS Motion	Yes	No

Figure 1-24: Summary of capabilities of SOLIDWORKS Simulation and SOLIDWORKS Motion with regard to analyzing discrete and distributed systems.

SOLIDWORKS Motion is intended to work with rigid bodies; SOLIDWORKS Simulation is intended to work with elastic bodies.

When a discrete system is analyzed in **SOLIDWORKS Simulation**, it is the user's responsibility to consider only those modes of vibration that are associated with the deformation of the discrete springs and not with the deformation of the assembly components.

SOLIDWORKS Motion and **SOLIDWORKS Simulation**, which are both **SOLIDWORKS** add-ins, serve different purposes and employ different modeling techniques. In **SOLIDWORKS Motion**, assembly mates are translated into kinematic pairs and assembly components become rigid links of a mechanism. Assembly mates that fully define an assembly must be suppressed in order to allow the motion of a mechanism. In **SOLIDWORKS Simulation**, assembly mates are ignored and restraints must be defined independently of the mates in the CAD model. Assembly components with touching faces are bonded unless specific contact conditions are defined.

Functionality of SOLIDWORKS Motion and SOLIDWORKS Simulation

As **SOLIDWORKS** add-ins, **Simulation** and **Motion** are connected to **SOLIDWORKS** CAD as well as between themselves. Connectivity and analysis capabilities are shown in Figure 1-25.

Figure 1-25: Types of analyses available in SOLIDWORKS Simulation and connectivity between SOLIDWORKS Simulation SOLIDWORKS Motion.

Results of SOLIDWORKS Motion may be transferred to SOLIDWORKS Simulation.

SOLIDWORKS Motion is not intended for vibration analysis and will not be used in this book. Most vibration problems in this book will be solved with **SOLIDWORKS Simulation** using the **Modal Superposition Method**. These will be problems of **Time Response, Frequency Response, Random Vibration** and **Response Spectrum**. Nonlinear vibration problems will be solved using the **Direct Integration Method**. We will provide in-depth descriptions of these types of analyses later, but now we have to address some important terminology issues.

Terminology issues

Terms used in **SOLIDWORKS Simulation** differ in many ways from terms you find in a standard textbook on vibration analysis. A summary of important differences along with short descriptions are given in Figure 1-26.

Textbook terminology	SOLIDWORKS Simulation study	Description
Linear Vibration Analysis	Linear Dynamic	All types of linear vibration analyses based on the Modal Superposition Method
Nonlinear Vibration Analysis	Nonlinear with Dynamic Option	Nonlinear vibration analysis Excitation is a function of time Results are functions of time
Modal	Frequency	Finds modes of vibration (frequency and shape)
Time Response	Modal Time History in linear analysis Nonlinear with Dynamic Option in nonlinear analysis	Excitation is a function of time Results are functions of time
Frequency Response	Harmonic	Excitation is harmonic and is defined as a function of frequency Results are functions of frequency
Random Vibration	Random	Excitation and results are in the form of Power Spectral Density
Response Spectrum	Response Spectrum Analysis	Base excitation in the form of a Response Spectrum
	Drop test	Nonlinear vibration analysis intended for drop test simulation

Figure 1-26: Summary of capabilities of SOLIDWORKS Simulation and SOLIDWORKS Motion.

Different types of vibration analysis will be described in the chapters that follow.

We will be alternating between standard textbook terminology and **SOLIDWORKS Simulation** terminology.

Definition of linear and nonlinear vibration studies in **Simulation** is shown in Figure 1-27.

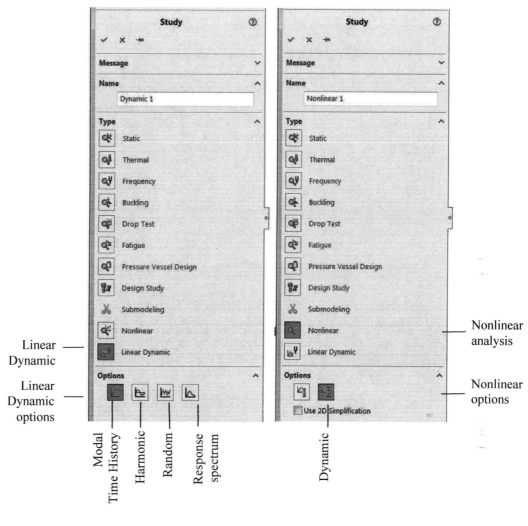

Linear vibration analysis   Nonlinear vibration analysis

Figure 1-27: Definition of linear and nonlinear vibration analysis studies in Simulation.

Different types of linear vibration studies are defined by selecting the analysis option. Nonlinear vibration study is defined as Nonlinear with Dynamic option.

2: Introduction to modal analysis

Topics covered

- ❏ Modal analysis
- ❏ Properties of a mode of vibration
- ❏ Interpreting results of modal analysis
- ❏ Normalizing displacement results in modal analysis

Modal analysis

Modal analysis, called a **Frequency** analysis in **Simulation**, finds natural frequencies and shapes of vibration that are associated with natural frequencies. **Modal** analysis assumes that the body vibrates in the absence of any excitation and damping. The vibration textbooks call this free undamped vibration.

Consider the simplest type of vibrating system: a **Single Degree of Freedom** oscillator (SDOF) with mass *m* and stiffness *k* which is vibrating in the absence of damping, excitation and gravity (Figure 2-1).

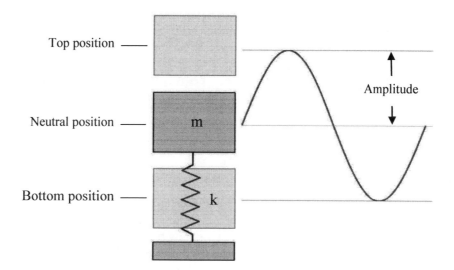

Figure 2-1: SDOF oscillator vibrating in the absence of damping and excitation. The problem is linear; mass m and stiffness k do not change during motion.

Vibration has been caused by an initial condition such as displacement and/or velocity.

The equation of motion of this SDOF can be derived by noticing that inertial forces equal stiffness force at any time (1). The displacement solution has the form of (2) where ω is the circular frequency of oscillations in radians per second (rad/s) and A is the amplitude of displacement. It is easy to prove that the equation of motion of the SDOF is satisfied for any A but only for one value of ω (3).

$$m\ddot{x} + kx = 0 \qquad (1)$$

$$x = A\sin(\omega t) \qquad (2)$$

$$\dot{x} = A\omega\cos(wt)$$

$$\ddot{x} = -A\omega^2\sin(\omega t)$$

$$m(-A\omega^2\sin(\omega t)) + k(A\sin(\omega t)) = 0$$

$$-mA\omega^2 + kA = 0$$

$$\omega = \sqrt{\frac{k}{m}} \qquad (3)$$

Frequency (3) is the natural frequency of an SDOF; this is the only frequency with which an SDOF can oscillate in the absence of excitation.

Review equation (1) and its solution (3) to notice a very important property of the natural frequency found here for an SDOF system but extendable to any vibrating system. When a system is vibrating with its natural frequency, there is a cancellation between inertial and stiffness forces. The resultant stiffness of an undamped system performing free, undamped vibration is therefore equal to **zero**. This happens for any amplitude of vibration.

Interpreting results of modal analysis

Modal analysis can only find the natural frequencies and the associated shapes (modes) of the analyzed structure performing free, undamped vibration. Since neither excitation nor damping is modeled in modal analysis, the modal analysis cannot provide any quantitative information on displacements and stresses. Displacement results can only be used to compare relative displacements between different portions of the analyzed structure and only within the same mode of vibration. We'll demonstrate this later when analyzing multi-degree of freedom systems.

In **SOLIDWORKS Simulation** displacement results of modal analysis are normalized to make the generalized mass matrix equal one (4).

$$\left| \varphi^T \right| \left\| M \right\| \left| \varphi \right| = \left| 1 \right|$$

φ eigenvector (shape of vibration)

φ^T transposed eigenvector   (4)

M   mass matrix

1   unit matrix

The effect of normalization can be demonstrated by running modal analysis on a model with the same geometry and modulus of elasticity but different material densities. This will be done using the BALL VALVE PLATE model. The material in the model is Cast Carbon Steel: restraints are shown in Figure 2-1. The geometry is simplified by omitting fillets.

Figure 2-2: BALL VALVE PLATE.

Fixed restraints are applied to both end faces of the shaft.

BALL VALVE PLATE features a simplified geometry where fillets have been removed. The sharp re-entrant edges would cause stress singularities if the model were used for stress analysis. If removal of fillets does not change the model stiffness significantly, this simplified geometry may be acceptable for modal analysis. The finite element mesh used in modal analysis should model stiffness correctly. If the model is not intended for subsequent stress analysis, geometry details that do not affect stiffness globally do not have to be modeled precisely since this will not affect the results of modal analysis.

Create a **Frequency** study titled *01 Cast Carbon Steel* as shown in Figure 2-3.

Figure 2-3: Properties of frequency study *01 Cast Carbon Steel.*

Only one mode of vibration will be found. One mode will suffice to demonstrate the effect of modal mass normalization.

Mesh the model using a **Standard Mesh** with second order solid elements of default size and define restraints as shown in Figure 2-2.

Displacement results of mode 1 are shown is Figure 2-4.

Node:	9789
X, Y, Z Location:	-250,20,7.08 mm
Value:	262

Node:	9738
X, Y, Z Location:	-177,20,-176 mm
Value:	165

AMPRES
262
240
218
196
175
153
131
109
87
65
44
22
0

Figure 2-4: Resultant displacement results in mode 1.

Color fringes along with a color legend are shown in the displacement results of modal analysis, but their numerical values are relatively valid only. For example, the ratio between resultant displacements in the probed locations is 262/165=1.59. Notice that probing disables the deformed shape.

Displacement results of modal analyses do not show any units to avoid a misinterpretation of results.

Numerical values of displacement results are normalized to make the modal mass equal to 1. Therefore, the displacement results will be different for the same model geometry and stiffness but different mass. To demonstrate this, we modify the original density of 7800kg/m³ and repeat the analysis with two custom materials:

1. Custom material 1: modulus of elasticity equal to that of Cast Carbon steel; mass density 780kg/m³

2. Custom material 2: modulus of elasticity equal to that of Cast Carbon steel; mass density of 78000kg/m³

Copy the frequency study *01 Cast Carbon Steel* into two new studies titled *02 10% Cast Carbon Steel* and *03 1000% Cast Carbon Steel*. Assign the corresponding custom materials as explained above. Obtain the results and summarize the displacements as shown in Figure 2-5.

780kg/m³ 7800kg/m³ 78000kg/m³

Figure 2-5: Displacement results in mode 1 for different materials.

Color legends are shown in the ascending order or mass density. The modal shape is the same for all material densities.

To gain a better insight on how displacement results are normalized in Modal analysis, we'll summarize the natural frequencies and the maximum displacement magnitudes for the different material densities listed in Figure 2-5. The summary is shown in Figure 2-6.

	Material density kg/m^3	Frequency of the first mode	Normalized max. displacement
1	780	1353Hz	829
2	7800	428Hz	262
3	78000	135Hz	83

Figure 2-6: summary of frequency and normalized displacement results for materials of different density.

Material density is modified by using a custom material.

When you review the results in Figure 2-6, remember that while the material density changes, the model stiffness remains the same. Even though this exercise has no relevance to real life, it still provides interesting results. As we know, a structure vibrating in a given mode of vibration may be treated as a **Single Degree of Freedom** oscillator (SDOF) with a natural frequency expressed by (2): $\omega = \sqrt{\dfrac{k}{m}}$

In our case stiffness remains the same; therefore, the natural frequency is inversely proportional to the square root of mass. This is why a 100 fold increase in the mass causes the frequency to drop to one tenth of the original frequency; compare frequency results in rows 1 and 3 in Figure 2-6.

Modal analysis normalizes the displacement results in such a way that the ratio of maximum displacements equals the inverse of the square root of the ratio of mass; compare displacement results in rows 1 and 3 in Figure 2-6.

Displacement results of modal analysis are so often misinterpreted that it may be better to show the results of modal analysis without colors, making it a deformation plot.

Read this message —

Deselect Show colors —

Figure 2-7: Plot of deformations in mode 1.

Deselecting colors eliminates color fringes and hides the color legend. This is often done to avoid misinterpretation of results.

The plot shows the shape of the first mode, material density 7800kg/m³.

To avoid misinterpretation of results modal analysis, the results may be normalized as shown in Figure 2-8.

Figure 2-8: Normalized plot of deformation in mode 1.

Normalizing displacement results is another method of avoiding misinterpretation of displacement results of modal analysis.

Summary of studies completed

Model	Configuration	Study Name	Study Type
BALL VALVE PLATE.sldprt	*Default*	*01 Cast Carbon Steel*	Frequency
		02 10% Cast Carbon Steel	Frequency
		03 1000% Cast Carbon Steel	Frequency

Figure 2-9: Names and types of studies completed in this chapter.

3: Modal analysis of distributed systems

Topics covered

- ❑ Modal analysis of distributed systems
- ❑ Meshing considerations in modal analysis
- ❑ Importance of mesh quality in modal analysis
- ❑ Importance of modeling supports
- ❑ Interpretation of results of modal analysis

The mode of vibration is a combination of frequency and shape; it depends on the stiffness and inertial properties of the analyzed structure. If finding modes of vibration is the only objective, geometry details such as notches or rounds don't have to be included in the analysis because they don't change the stiffness or inertia in a significant way. If the results of a modal analysis are used as pre-requisites to subsequent stress analyses, then the mesh has to comply with all requirements of the stress analyses.

To demonstrate the different requirements of the mesh in a stress and modal analysis, we will conduct both analyses on a simple model. Open part model NOTCH, make sure it is in configuration *02 notch* and observe the small round notch (Figure 3-1).

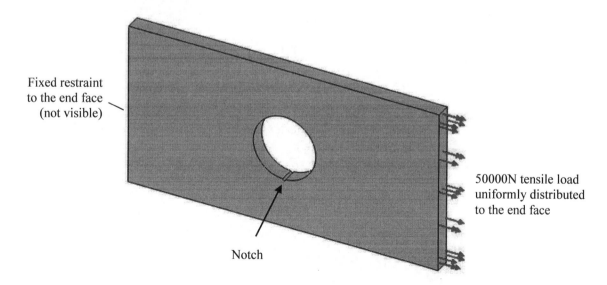

Fixed restraint to the end face (not visible)

50000N tensile load uniformly distributed to the end face

Notch

Figure 3-1: A notched hollow plate is subjected to tensile load and fixed restraint.

Restraint symbols are not shown.

A stress analysis of the NOTCH model requires careful preparation of the mesh. Create a **Static** study titled *01 stress* and define a mesh control on the notch face to assure correct element size and turn angle (Figure 3-2).

Figure 3-2: Mesh control defined on the face of the notch.

Element size on the controlled entity is 0.25mm; this is controlled independently of the global element size. Ratio defines the relative size of elements in consecutive layers in the transition zone between element size 0.25mm and global element size 5.27mm.

Define loads and restraints as shown in Figure 3-1 and obtain the solution. Next, copy study *01 stress* into a new study titled *02 stress*. Delete the mesh controls and obtain the solution with the default mesh. Von Mises stress results of both studies are shown in Figure 3-3.

Study *01 stress*
Correct stress results produced
by mesh with controls.
The maximum von Mises stress: 481MPa

Study *02 stress*
Incorrect stress results produced
by default mesh.
The maximum von Mises stress: 337MPa

Figure 3-3: Von Mises stress results produced with the correct mesh (left) and incorrect mesh (right).

Using the default element size and no mesh controls produces highly distorted elements that give incorrect stress results.

Compare the stress plots in Figure 3-3 and notice that the incorrect mesh returns an incorrect stress distribution pattern as well as von Mises stresses that are 25% lower as compared to the correct mesh. This quick review of stress analysis shows the importance of meshing small geometry details when stress results are sought.

We will now study the effects of the mesh on the results of modal analyses. Create two **Frequency** studies titled *03 modal* and *04 modal*. Define the same restraint as shown in Figure 3-1; don't define any load. In study *03 modal* use a mesh with the same controls as in study *01 stress*. In study *04 modal* don't use any mesh controls.

A summary of results of studies *03 modal* and *04 modal* is shown in Figure 3-4. The same figure also shows modal frequencies of a model without a notch. These results may be obtained by analyzing the model in configuration *01 no notch* using a default mesh; do this in study *05 modal*.

Mode number	Frequency [Hz]		
	Study *03 modal* Model with notch Mesh controls	Study *04 modal* Model with notch No mesh controls	Study *05 modal no notch* Model without notch No mesh controls
1	210.2	210.21	210.25
2	845.06	845.48	845.56
3	1274.4	1274.7	1275.3
4	1730.1	1730.1	1730.2
5	2825.7	2825.9	2826.1

Figure 3-4: Comparison of modal frequencies produced by the model with a notch and mesh controls, with a notch and no mesh controls, and without a notch.

Incorrect mesh or removal of the notch has next to no effect on natural frequencies.

The results summarized in Figure 3-4 show that incorrect meshing of small details or removing those details has little effect on the natural frequency. Animate any mode to see that the modal shapes also remain the same.

Stresses may be strongly dependent on small **local** features which must be correctly represented in a mesh intended for stress analysis. Modes of vibration depend on structural stiffness which is a **global** model property. Incorrect meshing or removal of small features does not change stiffness in a significant way. This is the reason that modal analysis is insensitive to incorrect meshing of small features or to the removal of these small features all together.

The above statement applies only if modal analysis is the only objective. If results of modal analysis are used as pre-requisites to subsequent vibration stress analyses, then all rigors of correct meshing apply to the modal analysis.

Stay with the *01 no notch* configuration open to perform a convergence analysis of natural frequencies. Copy study *05 modal* no notch into *06 modal no notch coarse* and mesh the model with a very coarse mesh using 25mm default element size. Then copy *05 modal no notch* into *07 modal no notch fine* and mesh the model with a very fine mesh using 2.5mm default element size. Frequency results in the first mode are shown in Figure 3-5.

Study *06 modal no notch coarse*
Element size 25mm
Frequency 213.2Hz

Study *05 modal no notch*
Element size 5.7mm
Frequency 210.3Hz

Study *07 modal no notch fine*
Element size 2.5mm
Frequency 210.1Hz

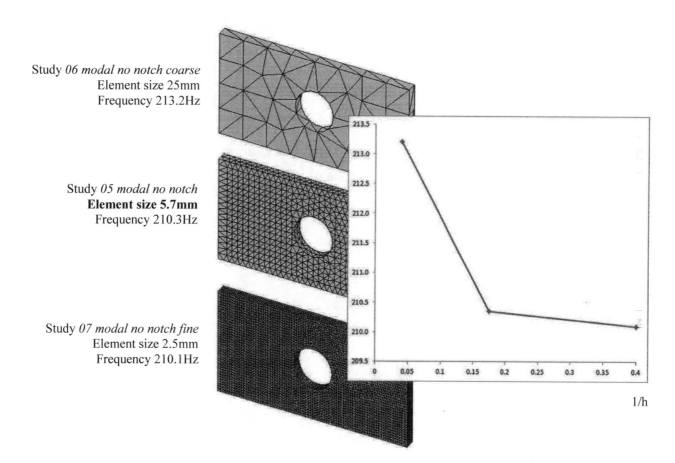

1/h

Figure 3-5: Frequency of the first mode as a function of 1/h, where h is the element size.

Frequency drops with element size and converges to the asymptotic value corresponding to a continuous model (model before discretization).

As Figure 3-5 indicates, the natural frequency converges to an asymptotic value. Remember that meshing adds stiffness to the model. The coarse mesh has more "artificial stiffness." With mesh refinement, as the artificial stiffness is gradually removed, the model becomes softer and, consequently, the natural frequency drops. In the limit, frequency tends to the asymptotic value that corresponds to a continuous model.

We have demonstrated this only for the first mode, but the same applies to all modes.

We'll return to the topic of artificial stiffness and its effect on modes of vibration in Chapter 4 discussing similarities and differences between modal and buckling analyses.

Summary of studies completed

Model	Configuration	Study Name	Study Type
NOTCH.sldprt	02 notch	01 stress	Static
		02 stress	Static
		03 modal	Frequency
		04 modal	Frequency
	01 no notch	05 modal no notch	Frequency
		06 modal no notch coarse	Frequency
		07 modal no notch fine	Frequency

Figure 3-6: Names and types of studies completed in this chapter.

4: Modal analysis – the effect of pre-stress

Topics covered

- ❏ Modal analysis with pre-stress
- ❏ Modal analysis and buckling analysis
- ❏ Artificial stiffness

If a structure is subjected to a load that produces significant tensile or compressive stresses, those stresses may significantly change the structure's stiffness and consequently, its modes of vibration. To account for that change, modal analysis needs to be completed on a structure with a modified stiffness caused by the existing state of stress. This type of modal analysis, called pre-load or pre-stress modal analysis, is conducted in two steps. First, a static analysis is run to find stresses that develop due to a load; these stresses are used to modify the structure's stiffness. Next, modal analysis is run on the structure with the stiffness modified by the previously found stresses.

Predominantly, tensile stresses will increase the natural frequencies as is illustrated by tuning a guitar string or stress-stiffening of a rotating component like a turbine blade. Rotating machinery typically requires that the effect of pre-stress be considered. Compressive stresses on the other hand will decrease natural frequencies. In this chapter we will illustrate the effect of tensile and compressive stresses on natural frequencies. Then we will demonstrate how a modal analysis with pre-stress relates to a buckling analysis.

Open part model ROTOR which is a simplified representation of a helicopter rotor. We are interested in the effect of centrifugal forces that develop due to rotor rotation on the fundamental natural frequency of the rotor blade. The fundamental frequency is the lowest natural frequency. All four blades are identical and isolated from each other by a support at the hub. Therefore, we may simplify the analysis to only one blade (Figure 4-1).

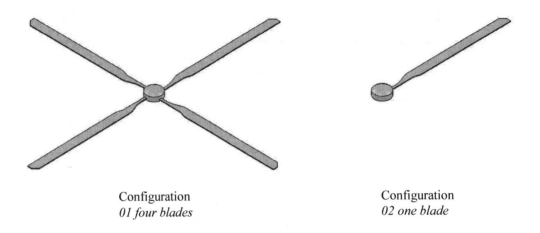

Configuration
01 four blades

Configuration
02 one blade

Figure 4-1: ROTOR model.

Modal analysis can be conducted on one blade.

Switch to *02 one blade* configuration and create a **Frequency** study *01 rotating*. Apply **Fixed** restraints as shown in Figure 4-2.

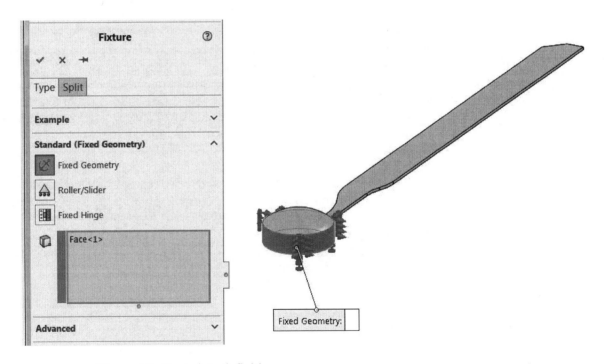

Figure 4-2: Restraints definition.

A fixed restraint is defined to the cylindrical surface. You may also apply it to the top and bottom face of the hub; it won't have any significant effect on the vibration of the blade.

Define a centrifugal load of 300RPM by selecting the cylindrical surface where the **Fixed** restraint has been defined. This cylindrical face uniquely defines the axis which is taken as the axis of rotation as shown in Figure 4-3.

Figure 4-3: Centrifugal load definition.

A centrifugal load is defined by an angular rotation about the axis. Use metric units to define it in revolutions per minute (RPM). Do not define any angular acceleration.

Vibration Analysis with SOLIDWORKS Simulation 2016

In the study properties, specify one mode and use the **Direct sparse** solver (Figure 4-4).

One mode —

Direct sparse solver —

Figure 4-4: Properties of the frequency study.

Direct sparse solver must be used; FFEPlus solver is not available for modal analysis with pre-stress.

Mesh the model with the default mesh size and solve the study. Copy study *01 rotating* into *02 stopped*, suppress the centrifugal load and solve the study without pre-stress.

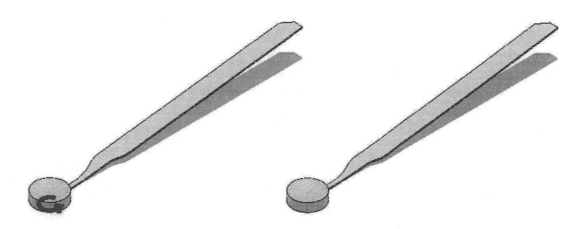

Fundamental frequency
of rotating blade: 5.35Hz

Fundamental frequency
of stopped blade: 0.54Hz

Figure 4-5: The first mode of vibration of rotating and stopped blade.

The mode shape is the same for the rotating and stopped blade; the modal frequency is very different. Both plots show the undeformed shape superimposed on the modal plot.

A comparison of results between rotating and stopped blade shows a very strong effect of rotation; the first natural frequency is ten times as high for the rotating blade as it is for the stopped blade. The centrifugal force produces tensile stresses which cause stress stiffening of the blade. The resultant stiffness of the rotating blade is the sum of the elastic stiffness and stress stiffness. Stress stiffness due to tensile stress is positive, and the resultant stiffness of the rotating blade is higher than the stiffness of the stationary blade. Higher stiffness, in turn, produces a higher natural frequency.

When a load is present in a **Frequency** study, this load is used to modify the stiffness. The analysis is then called modal analysis with pre-load. The term modal analysis with pre-stress is also used. The solution progresses in two steps. First, a static analysis is run to find stresses. These stresses are used to modify the model stiffness. Then modal analysis is run using the combined elastic and stress stiffness.

Remember that it is a serious error to confuse pre-load with excitation load!

The effect of tensile stress on the natural frequency may be easily demonstrated by tuning a guitar string, where increasing string tension increases the natural frequency.

The effect of compressive stresses on the natural frequency is the opposite; compressive stresses produce negative stress stiffness which decreases the resultant stiffness and the natural frequency decreases.

We will demonstrate this with the COLUMN model subjected to compression by two wedges as shown in Figure 4-6. This illustration schematically shows an apparatus used to demonstrate buckling of a rectangular column.

Figure 4-6: A prismatic column compressed by two wedges.

The left wedge is fixed. The right wedge is held in between rollers. It can only translate in the direction of the load.

The column shown here is shorter than the column in the COLUMN assembly model.

The column is "squeezed" between to wedges; one wedge is fixed and provides support, the other one is guided by rollers and can move only in the direction of the load. We want to simulate this test rig to find a relation between the applied load and the first natural frequency of the loaded column in the range of the load magnitude changing from a tensile load to a compressive load up to the point of buckling. Using the test rig as shown in Figure 4-6 we would not be able to apply a tensile load, but using **SOLIDWORKS Simulation**, this is very easy. The analysis does not require analysis of an assembly; it can be completed on one part.

For your information, review the COLUMN assembly model, then open the COLUMN part model which will be used for analysis.

To find the magnitude of the buckling load we need to run a buckling analysis. Using the COLUMN part model, create a **Buckling** study titled *00 buckling* and define restraints as shown in Figure 4-7.

A fixed restraint on the split line on the end face (line not visible).

Restraint to the split line on the end face in the direction normal to the Top reference plane.

Figure 4-7: Restraints applied to the COLUMN model.

The fixture window shows restraint on the side of the moving wedge. Restraint on the side of fixed wedge is a fixed restraint. The fixed restraint window is not shown.

Notice that the **Fixed** restraint, as defined on the split line on the side of the fixed wedge, will be transferred to nodes of solid elements which have three degrees of freedom. Therefore, this **Fixed** restraint will effectively produce a hinge support.

Next, define a load as shown in Figure 4-8.

Figure 4-8: Load applied to the COLUMN model.

The load is applied to the same split line where the restraint on the side of moving wedge has been applied.

Notice that on the loaded end, the restraint and load are both applied to the same entity (the split line), but in different directions. If the load was applied in the direction of this restraint it would be ineffective.

Mesh the model with the default element size and run the solution of the buckling study. The first buckling mode is shown in Figure 4-9 and the **Buckling Load Factor** (BLF) is 1.5755, meaning that according to the linear buckling model, buckling will happen at a load of 1575.5N.

Select
Normalize
Mode
Shape

<u>Figure 4-9: Buckled shape shown using displacement plot; undeformed model
is superimposed on the deformed plot.</u>

*Even though numerical values are shown, their values may be used only to
find a displacement ratio rather than absolute displacement. This is in close
analogy to modal analysis. In this plot, the numerical values have been
normalized.*

The linear buckling analysis was necessary to establish the range of loads in
the modal analysis with pre-stress. We'll now conduct a numerical experiment
subjecting the model to different loads ranging from tensile to compressive to
study the effect of pre-load on the fundamental natural frequency. The
experiment will be conducted in twelve **Simulation** studies while the load is
changed from a 1500N tensile load, to a compressive load causing buckling.
A tensile load is denoted as positive, compressive as negative.

We should point out that numerical results presented in this experiment may
differ slightly depending on the service pack used. In all cases the **Direct
sparse solver** is used.

Create a **Frequency** study titled *01*; you may copy loads, restraints and the mesh from *00 buckling*. Remember to reverse the load direction to tensile and make it 1500N. Obtain the solution and record the first natural frequency. Next, proceed in load steps shown in Figure 4-10.

Study number	Preload N	Frequency Hz
01	+1500	177.88
02	+1000	162.78
03	+500	146.12
04	0	127.31
05	-500	105.19
06	-1000	76.95
07	-1200	62.15
08	-1400	42.49
09	-1500	27.89
10	-1550	16.20
11	-1570	7.52
12	-1575.49	0.29

Figure 4-10: A summary of the 12 studies illustrates the change of the first natural frequency with the applied pre-load. All runs are solved with the default element size of 3.11mm.

Plus (+) sign indicated tensile load, minus (-) sign indicated compressive load.

Review the results in Figure 4-10 and notice that the compressive pre-load in study 12 is just 0.01N less than the bucking load.

Results summarized in the above table are presented as a graph in Figure 4-11. A very steep curve near the buckling load is why the last four steps were conducted with small load increments.

Figure 4-11: Frequency of the first mode of vibration as a function of pre-load.

The frequency reaches zero when the compressive load equals the buckling load.

As Figure 4-11 shows, a pre-load causing the drop of the first natural frequency to zero is equal to the buckling load.

Tensile stresses develop positive stress stiffness that adds up to the elastic stiffness; therefore, the resultant stiffness increases, which is reflected by a higher natural frequency as compared to the unloaded column. Compressive stresses develop negative stress stiffness that is subtracted from the elastic stiffness and this decreases the resultant stiffness; consequently the natural frequency decreases. When the pre-load approaches the magnitude of buckling load, the resultant stiffness is very low producing a very low natural frequency. When the pre-load reaches the buckling load, the stiffness drops down to zero and that leads to buckling.

When the magnitude of a compressive load approaches the buckling load, the effective stiffness is very close to zero; this is why it has a near-zero natural frequency. Therefore, we may use the model from study *12*, the one pre-loaded with a 1575.49N compressive load, as a tool to investigate the effect of discretization on the model stiffness. As you know, meshing adds some stiffness to a model; let's call it artificial stiffness. The larger the elements are, the more artificial stiffness is added and vice versa. The artificial stiffness does not change with pre-load; therefore, in study *12*, the artificial stiffness is a major contributor to the model stiffness. The natural frequency of 0.31Hz is not a real frequency under that load. Elastic stiffness and stress stiffness have almost canceled themselves out and this 0.31Hz frequency is an artifact produced by the artificial stiffness that is there due to discretization error. The numerical value of that frequency completely depends on the choice of mesh size.

We will now conduct a numerical experiment to demonstrate that the remaining model stiffness in study *12* is a product of discretization, and not a real stiffness.

Keeping in mind that all twelve studies were run with default element size 3.1mm, we will now use 2mm element size. Copy study *12* into *12 fine* and re-mesh it with a 2mm element size. With a smaller element size, the artificial stiffness is reduced and the effective stiffness becomes negative. An attempt to run the solution produces an error message shown in Figure 4-12.

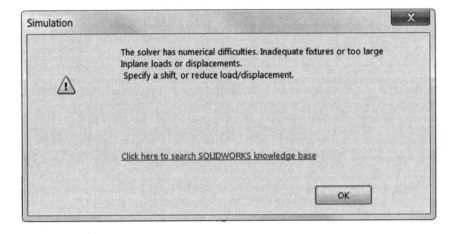

Figure 4-12: Error message caused by a negative effective stiffness.

The explanation offered by the error message is generic and does not apply to our problem.

We now realize that all that was "holding" the model stable in study *12* was the artificial stiffness produced by the process of discretization. The contribution of artificial stiffness to total stiffness is significant only for loads very close to buckling because the real stiffness is then very low.

As an additional exercise, you may want to analyze the effect of element size on the natural frequency in the model subjected to a compressive load that is very close to the buckling load. You'll find that the natural frequency strongly depends on the element size as shown in Figure 4-13.

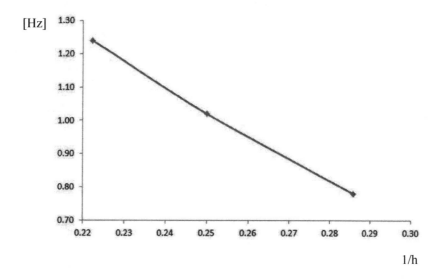

Figure 4-13: Natural frequency at the compressive load of 1575.49N as a function of the inverse of element size *h*.

A strong dependence of frequency on the element size makes these results useless.

A fundamental rule of using FEA results states that before we use results to make a design decision, we must prove that these results are not significantly dependent on the choice of discretization (element size). The graph in Figure 4-13 proves the opposite: frequency results for load magnitudes close to buckling are strongly dependent on the mesh size.

Summary of studies completed

Model	Configuration	Study Name	Study Type
ROTOR.sldprt	02 one blade	01 rotating	Frequency
		02 stopped	Frequency
COLUMN.sldprt	Default	00 buckling	Buckling
		01	Frequency
		02	Frequency
		03	Frequency
		04	Frequency
		05	Frequency
		06	Frequency
		07	Frequency
		08	Frequency
		09	Frequency
		10	Frequency
		11	Frequency
		12	Frequency
		12 fine	Frequency

Figure 4-14: Names and types of studies completed in this chapter.

5: Modal analysis - properties of lower and higher modes

Topics covered

- ❑ Modal analysis using shell elements
- ❑ Properties of lower and higher modes
- ❑ Convergence of frequencies with mesh refinement

Consider a bracket supported by two hinges along both ends. Open the U BRACKET part model and notice that the bracket is modeled as a surface (Figure 5-1).

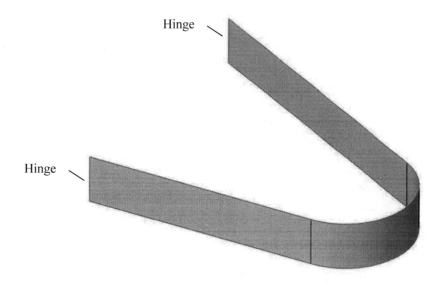

Figure 5-1: U BRACKET model supported by two hinges.

The geometry is represented by a surface. Therefore the thickness is missing from geometry.

Create a **Frequency** study *01 default mesh* and define a shell thickness of 2mm (Figure 5-2).

Figure 5-2: Shell thickness definition.

Mid-surface means that thickness is symmetric about the surface.

Define restraints as shown in Figure 5-3.

Immovable —

Figure 5-3: Hinge restraints.

Use Immovable restraints to allow hinging about the two short ends.

Notice that the **Fixture** window differentiates between **Fixed Geometry** and **Immovable (No translation)** restraints. This is because the model geometry is a surface, and **Simulation** recognizes it as a candidate for meshing with shell elements.

Mesh the model using the default settings (Figure 5-4).

Figure 5-4: U BRACKET meshed with shell elements.

Colors (not visible in this black and white illustration) differentiate between the top and bottom of shell elements. Here, the outside is meshed with tops; the shell's normal vector goes from inside to outside the model.

Shell element orientation is very important in stress analysis. Different stress results are reported on different sides of shell elements. In modal analysis, which does not calculate stress, shell orientation has no impact on results. This is of course correct only if modal analysis is our only objective. If it is followed by vibration analysis where stresses need to be analyzed, then the orientation of shell elements must be carefully controlled.

Obtain a solution for 10 modes of vibration and review the results as shown in Figure 5-5.

User defined scale

Colors deselected

Mode 1: 112Hz   Mode 2: 332Hz

Mode 3: 614Hz   Mode 4: 682Hz

Figure 5-5: The first four modes of U BRACKET.

The undeformed model shape is shown along with the deformed model. To differentiate the undeformed shape from the modal shape, the scale of deformation has been adjusted individually for each mode. The Mode Shape window shows the deformation scale adjusted for Mode 1. Colors are deselected.

A review of shapes of all calculated modes reveals the following qualitative properties of lower and higher modes. Lower modes "find" the easiest way to move structure; notice that the bracket vibrating in mode 1 hinges about supports; little deformation is present. Higher modes have progressively complex shapes while motion tends to be "more uniformly" distributed over the model.

The above findings indicate the following:

- Lower modes tend to maximize kinetic energy and minimize strain energy of a vibrating structure.
- Higher modes tend to maximize strain energy and minimize kinetic energy.

While the second statement is easy to prove just by observing modal shapes, the first one can't be proven by watching modal shapes because displacement results are normalized and are not comparable between different modes. Vibration analysis following modal analysis is required to demonstrate higher displacement amplitudes of lower modes.

The U BRACKET model is numerically efficient (solution is fast) because of its simplicity and because it uses shell elements. This makes it a convenient tool to demonstrate the effect of mesh refinement on the natural frequency already discussed in the previous chapter.

Copy study *01 default mesh* into three studies: *02 10mm, 03 5mm, 04 2mm*. In each study mesh the model with element size indicated by the study name. Obtain frequency results for meshes with element sizes of 10mm, 5mm, and 2mm. The graph in Figure 5-6 demonstrates the convergence of the first frequency.

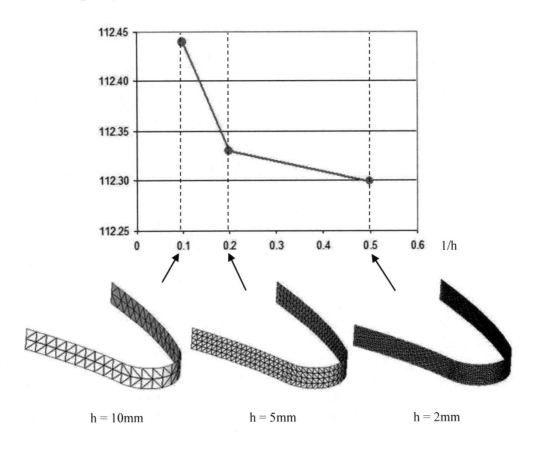

h = 10mm   h = 5mm   h = 2mm

Figure 5-6: Convergence of the frequency of the first mode.

The graph shows the frequency as a function of 1/h where h is the element size.

The effect of mesh density is not strong, but noticeable.

Summary of studies completed

Model	Configuration	Study Name	Study Type
U BRACKET.sldprt	*Default*	*01 default mesh*	Frequency
		02 10mm	Frequency
		03 5mm	Frequency
		04 2mm	Frequency

Figure 5-7: Names and types of studies completed in this chapter.

6: Modal analysis – mass participation, properties of modes

Topics covered

- ❏ Modal mass
- ❏ Modal mass participation
- ❏ Modes of vibration of axisymmetric structures
- ❏ Modeling bearing restraints
- ❏ Using modal analysis to find "weak spots"

Procedure

We'll analyze the SHAFT assembly model which is a simplified representation of a shaft with two gears, supported by two spherical bearings that allow for some angular displacement. Many small features that are not essential for modal analysis (chamfers, rounds, undercuts) are not present in this model. They would have to be included if we had to conduct stress analysis.

Large gear

Small gear

Bearing

Bearing

Figure 6-1: SHAFT supported by two spherical bearings.

Many features important for manufacturing, assembly and function are not included in this model; Teeth are modeled only schematically.

The model is shown in the 01 bearings configuration. The center of mass of the assembly is shown.

The objective of this exercise is to find the first few natural frequencies of the shaft supported by spherical bearings, and to compare these results with results of the shaft when unsupported. This exercise introduces vibration properties of axi-symmetric structures, modal mass participation and the effect of restraints on the mass participating in vibration. The major modeling consideration is modeling supports that allow for angular displacement present in spherical bearing supports.

The SHAFT assembly model has three configurations: *01 bearing, 02 no bearings,* and *03 spherical bearing faces*. Configuration *01 bearings* serves only to illustrate the problem. Notice that applying restraints to cylindrical faces of two bearings would eliminate rotations allowed by the spherical bearings. The difference between a fixed bearing support and a spherical bearing support is easy to explain if we consider modes of vibration of a beam with fixed supports and simple supports.

Fixed support on both sides

Simple support on both sides

Figure 6-2: Bending mode shape of a beam with fixed supports (top) and simple supports (bottom).

The ends of the beam with simple supports are able to rotate.

The model used to create plots in Figure 6-2 is called BEAM DEMO. It is not directly related to SHAFT exercise.

The difference between fixed and simple supports is easy to model using beam elements, as shown in the BEAM DEMO model. These two types of supports are differentiated in BEAM DEMO by selecting either **Fixed** or **Immovable** restraints.

In the case of the SHAFT model where restraints can't be applied to one point, we'll need to use a **Bearing Support** as shown in Figure 6-3.

Change the model configuration to *02 no bearings*, create a **Frequency** study titled *01 bearing support* and define **Bearing Fixture** restraints as shown in Figure 6-3.

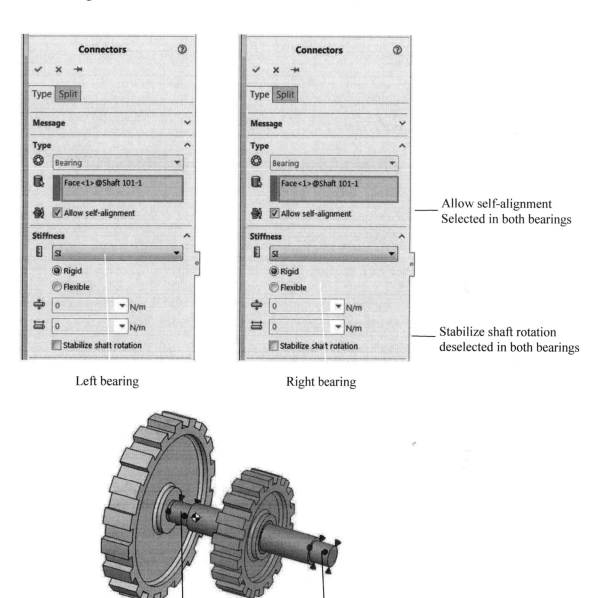

Left bearing   Right bearing

Allow self-alignment
Selected in both bearings

Stabilize shaft rotation
deselected in both bearings

Left bearing   Right bearing

Figure 6-3: Bearing Support.

Bearing supports must be defined individually for each side. Definitions of left bearing and right bearing support are identical.

Since the shaft rotation is not restrained, the model will have one **Rigid Body Mode** – rotation about its axis.

Specify 16 modes in the study properties. Mesh the model with default element size and obtain solution.

Follow steps in Figure 6-4 to display a list of natural frequencies.

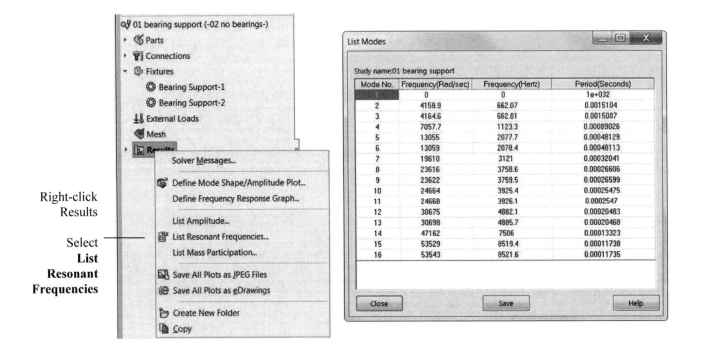

<u>Figure 6-4: List Modes table shows the natural frequencies.</u>

Frequencies are listed in the ascending order.

Modal frequencies in Figure 6-4 are shown using three units:

rad/s, Hz, and s.

The relation between frequency ω *(rad/s)* and *f (Hz)* is: $\omega = 2\Pi f$

The relation between frequency *f (Hz)* and vibration period T is: $T = 1/f$

A short note on a terminology issue: the pop-up menu in Figure 6-4 shows command **List Resonant Frequencies**. This should be called List Modal Frequencies because a resonant frequency and modal frequency are not the same even though these terms are used interchangeably. The modal frequency is found in the absence of damping; the resonant frequency is affected by damping.

Frequency and shape are not the only factors defining mode of vibration. Another very important characteristic is the **Mass Participation**; it indicates what percentage of the total mass participates in vibration in the given mode. Follow steps in Figure 6-5 to look into **Mass Participation** in all 16 modes found in the SHAFT assembly.

Review all three graphs that can be constructed with **Define Frequency Response Graph**.

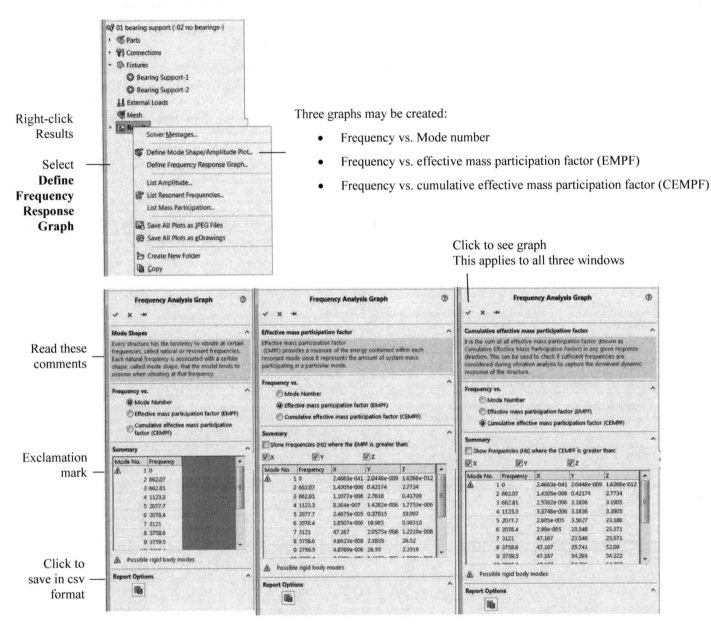

Right-click
Results

Select
**Define
Frequency
Response
Graph**

Three graphs may be created:

- Frequency vs. Mode number
- Frequency vs. effective mass participation factor (EMPF)
- Frequency vs. cumulative effective mass participation factor (CEMPF)

Click to see graph
This applies to all three windows

Read these
comments

Exclamation
mark

Click to
save in csv
format

Frequency vs. Mode number

Frequency vs. effective mass
participation factor (**EMPF**)

Frequency vs. cumulative effective
mass participation factor (**CEMPF**)

Figure 6-5: Frequency Analysis Graph windows in three options.

*The table in Frequency vs. Mode number window is a repetition of Figure 6-4.
Each window can be shown as a graph and/or saved in the csv format for
processing in Excel. Exclamation mark indicates that RBMs have been
detected by the solver.*

You may examine the **Modal Mass Participation** in x, y, z directions by reviewing the automatically created graphs or you may export data in the csv format to Excel and construct your own graphs as shown in Figure 6-6.

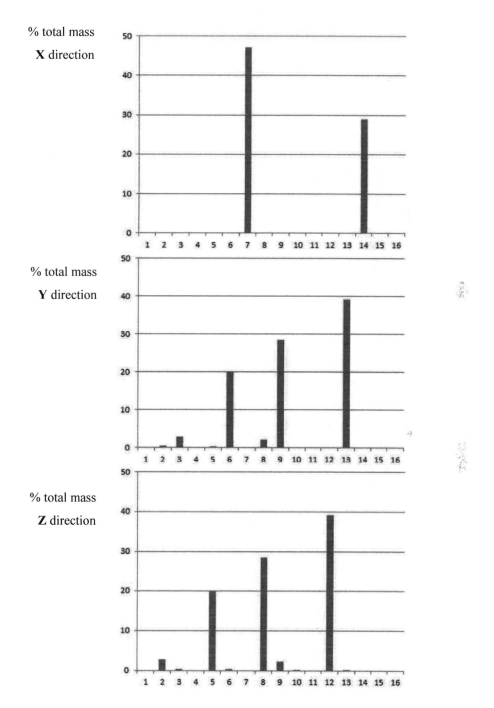

Figure 6-6: Effective mass participation factor in X, Y, Z directions is shown on ordinate; mode number is shown on abscissa.

The modes shown here are listed in the table Frequency vs. Mode number in Figure 6-5.

Animate the modes with significant mass participation in X direction as shown in Figure 6-6. These are modes 7 and 14; notice that this numbering includes the Rigid Body Mode which is counted as mode 1.

Mode 7: 3121Hz   Mode 14: 7506Hz

Figure 6-7: Shapes and frequencies of mode 7 and mode 14. These modes have significant mass participations in X direction.

Mode 7 is associated with deformation of the large gear; mode 14 is associated with deformation of small gear.

Review of animated modes 7 and 14 clearly shows mass moving in X direction. Notice that the shaft is unlikely to be excited in X direction. Therefore, these modes may never manifest themselves, especially mode 14 which has a very high frequency.

Now animate these modes that have significant mass participation in Y and Z directions. These are modes 2 and 3, 5 and 6, 8 and 9, 12 and 13.

Shapes and frequencies of mode 8 and mode 9 are shown in Figure 6-8.

Mode 8: 3758.6Hz   Mode 9: 3759.5Hz

Figure 6-8: Shapes and frequencies of mode 8 and mode 9; both are bending modes.

Mode 8 is associated with deformation of shaft in XZ plane; it has significant mass participation in Z direction.

Mode 9 is associated with deformation of shaft in XY plane; it has significant mass participation in Y direction.

Animate modes 2 and 3, 5 and 6, 12 and 13 before proceeding.

We may use the modal results shown in Figure 6-8 to make important observations about modal frequencies and shapes of the SHAFT model.

Look at four pairs of modes: 2 and 3, 5 and 6, 8 and 9, 12 and 13.They are all bending modes in XY and XZ planes; all these modes are associated with rotation about the centers of the bearings; the results are summarized in Figure 6-9.

	Mode number	Frequency [Hz]	Plane of motion
Pair 1	2	662.07	XZ
	3	662.81	XY
Pair 2	5	2077.7	XZ
	6	2078.4	XY
Pair 3	8	3758.6	XZ
	9	3759.5	XY
Pair 4	12	4882.1	XZ
	13	4885.7	XY

Figure 6-9: Frequencies of four pairs of modes identified as bending modes in XY and XZ planes.

Each pair has almost the same frequency. Animation indicates that modal shapes are identical but rotated by 90° about the X axis.

Identical modal shapes and almost identical frequencies are not coincidental. Repetitive modes with the plane of vibration rotated by 90° characterize modal results of axi-symmetric structures. These modes are called coupled modes. A small difference in the numerical value of frequency is caused by teeth and by discretization error. Teeth make the model not perfectly axi-symmetric; discretization error also makes the stiffness of the finite element model not perfectly axi-symmetric.

Animate the modal shapes of coupled modes to confirm that the shapes are indeed identical but rotated by 90° (Figure 6-8). Notice that modal shapes are not exactly aligned with XZ and XY planes. An alignment of bending modes shape with the global coordinate system is not a rule for analysis of axi-symmetric problems.

Next, animate mode 4 which has no significant mass participations in any direction. Shape and frequency of mode 4 are shown in Figure 6-10.

Mode 4: 1123.3Hz

<u>Figure 6-10: Shape and frequency of mode 4; this mode has no significant mass participation in any of the principal directions.</u>

This is a torsional mode; two gears rotate in the opposite directions about the axis of the shaft while the connecting shaft experiences torsion.

Finally, animate mode 1 which is the **Rigid Body Mode**; its modal shape shows that SHAFT assembly rotates as a rigid body about its axis (Figure 6-11).

Mode 1: 0Hz

Figure 6-11: Shape and frequency of the Rigid Body Mode 1.

Frequency 0Hz is assigned to rigid body modes by solver.

Shapes of the torsional mode 4 (Figure 6-10) and the rigid body mode 1 (Figure 6-11) look the same in black and white illustrations; you need to animate them in **Simulation** to see differences. When animated, the shapes of modes 1 and 4 are easy to observe because of teeth. This is why the assembly model SHAFT features schematically modeled teeth. Modal shapes 4 and 1 would be impossible to observe if teeth were not modeled.

The **Cumulative effective mass participation factor (CEMPF)** (Figure 6-5) in X, Y, and Z directions in each mode is the sum of the values of **Effective participation factors** (EMPF) up to and including that mode.

In continuation of SHAFT exercise we will compare the shape of frequency of the first bending mode between SHAFT assembly supported by bearings and unsupported SHAFT assembly. Copy study *01 bearing support* into *02 no supports*, delete or suppress bearing support and obtain solution; the solution will show six rigid body modes. The first elastic model will be mode 7 which is a torsional mode; mode 8 will be the first bending mode. Therefore, the comparison needs to be done between mode 2 of the model with bearing supports and mode 8 of the unsupported model.

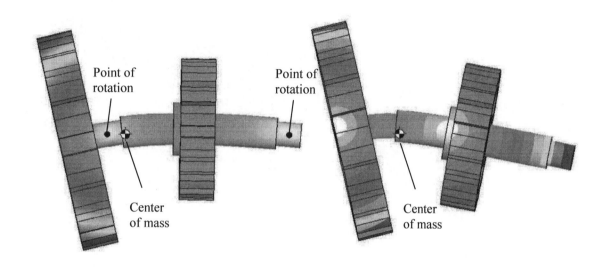

Spherical bearings support

Mode 2
Frequency: 662Hz

Vibration takes place about
the spherical bearings.

No supports

Mode 8
Frequency: 845Hz

Vibration takes place about the
centre of mass.

Figure 6-12: Comparison of the first bending mode of SHAFT with bearing supports and unsupported.

The center of mass symbol may be inserted into assembly as a reference geometry.

In the absence of supports, vibration always takes place about the center of mass. Removal of the bearing supports affects the model stiffness, and mass participation. The combined effect of both changes results in the increase of the frequency of the first bending mode.

The SHAFT model can also be used to illustrate that modal analysis provides a qualitative review of "weak spots." While absolute displacements can't be found in modal analysis, the relative displacements are valid. Return to configuration *01 bearing support* and animate bending mode 2 and bending mode 8 of the model supported by spherical bearings. Observe bending of the small cantilever shaft holding the large gear. This animation reveals a potential design fault: the heavy gear held by a soft cantilever shaft (Figure 6-13).

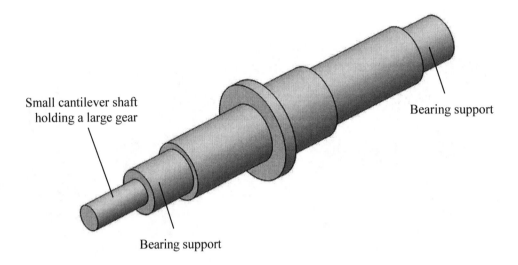

Small cantilever shaft holding a large gear

Bearing support

Bearing support

Figure 6-13: Potential design flaw identified by modal analysis: a soft cantilever beam supports a heavy gear.

The split face used to define a bearing support near the large gear is not shown in this illustration.

The flexibility of the large gear sitting on the small cantilever shaft may cause alignment problems, noise and premature wear. Therefore, based on the results of this analysis, the designer may decide to move the bearing to the end of the shaft.

We used a **Bearing Support** to provide the model with the ability to perform rotations about the bearings even though bearings themselves were not included in the model. The same support may be represented if bearings are added to the assembly and their outside face is modeled spherically as in assembly configuration *03 spherical bearing faces.*

Figure 6-14 shows the **On Spherical Faces** restraints defined for both bearings; this is equivalent to the **Bearing Support** with **Allow Self-alignment** selected as shown in Figure 6-3.

Translations in the radial direction are suppressed on both spherical faces

Figure 6-14: Bearing supports modeled using restraints defined in local spherical coordinate systems.

This restraint has to be defined individually for each bearing.

Switch to *03 spherical bearing faces* configuration and create **Frequency** study *03 spherical*. Analyze the model with restraints defined as shown in Figure 6-14 and verify that the results are close to those obtained using **Bearing Supports**. The slight difference is due to the fact that the model shown in Figure 6-14 takes into consideration the inertial effects of the bearings.

Summary of studies completed

Model	Configuration	Study Name	Study Type
BEAM DEMO.sldprt	*Default*	*01 Fixed*	Frequency
		02 Immovable	Frequency
SHAFT.sldasm	*02 no bearings*	*01 bearing support*	Frequency
		02 no support	Frequency
	03 spherical bearing faces	*03 spherical*	Frequency

Figure 6-15: Names and types of studies completed in this chapter.

7: Modal analysis – mode separation

Topics covered

- ❑ Modal analysis with shell elements
- ❑ Modes of vibration of symmetric structures
- ❑ Symmetry boundary conditions in modal analysis
- ❑ Anti-symmetry boundary condition in modal analysis

Procedure

The CAR model is a simplified representation of a car body; we'll use it to find the first torsional mode of vibration. Frequency of the first torsional mode is an important factor in vehicle handling and ride quality. Modern uni-body sedans have the first torsional frequency in the range 25-30Hz. Convertibles have "softer" bodies and, consequently, a much lower torsional frequency of 10-15Hz.

Due to a schematic representation of the car body design, the CAR model will not return realistic numerical values of natural frequencies. Still, it will allow us to review important modeling techniques used in modal analysis.

Review the CAR model in its two configurations *01 full* and *02 half* (Figure 7-1).

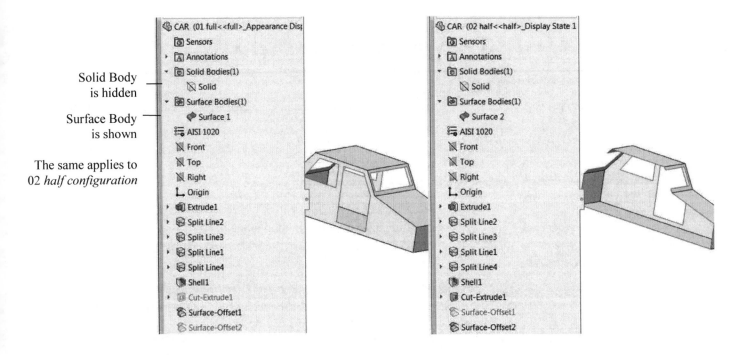

Solid Body is hidden

Surface Body is shown

The same applies to 02 *half configuration*

01 full configuration   *02 half* configuration

Solid bodies folder and Surface bodies folders are shown

Figure 7-1: Controlling display of Solid Bodies and Surface Bodies folders. The CAR model consists of Solid Body and Surface body; the Solid Body is hidden.

To show the Solid Bodies and Surface Bodies folders in the SOLIDWORKS Feature Manager Design Tree, right click anywhere in the Feature Manage window and use the pop-up window to show these items. Do not confuse show/hide of Solid Bodies folder and Surface Bodies folder in the Feature Manager Design Tree with show/hide of actual Solid or Surface bodies which are held in these folders.

Activate the *01 full* configuration and create a **Frequency** study called *01 full*. In the study properties, request 12 modes to be found. Exclude the **Solid Body** from the analysis as shown in Figure 7-2.

Right-click
SolidBody, select
Exclude from
Analysis.

Figure 7-2: Solid Body must be excluded from the analysis to avoid meshing of the Solid Body.

Even though the Solid Body has been hidden in the CAD model, it still has to be removed from analysis.

Right-click **Surface Body**, select **Edit Definition** and enter a shell element thickness of 50mm (we do not attempt to model a car body realistically).

Obtain the solution using the default element size and review frequencies of all modes; follow steps shown in Figure 7-3.

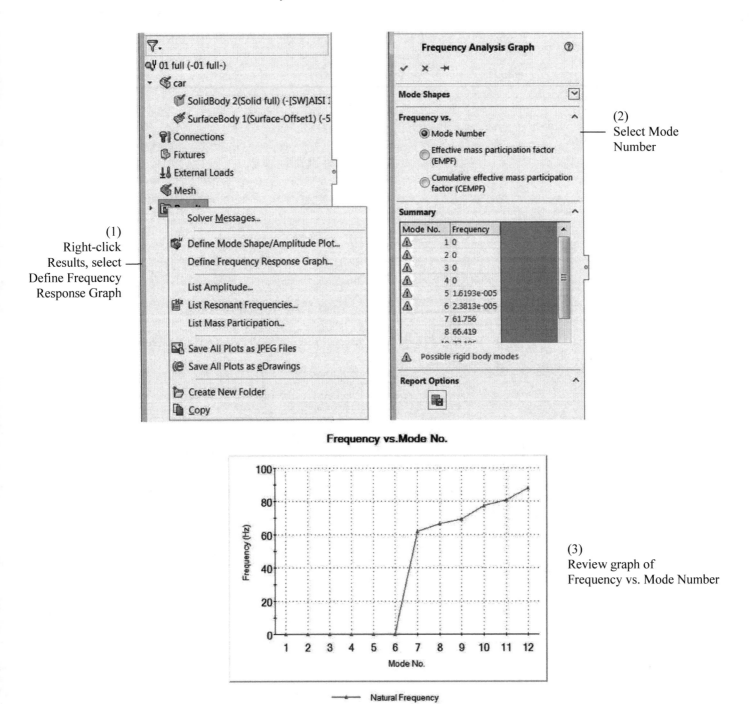

Figure 7-3: In the absence of restraints, the first six modes are Rigid Body Modes with frequencies very close to or equal to 0Hz.

Modes 5 and 6 are not exactly zero due to discretization error. Frequency vs. Mode Number graph has been created automatically. Lines between points have no meaning; therefore, points in the graph should not be connected. Export this graph to Excel and re-construct it as a bar graph.

Animate the six elastic modes (modes 7-12) and notice that the second elastic mode of vibration, which is mode number 8, is the torsional mode we are looking for. Also, observe that the deformed shapes are either symmetric or anti-symmetric (Figure 7-4).

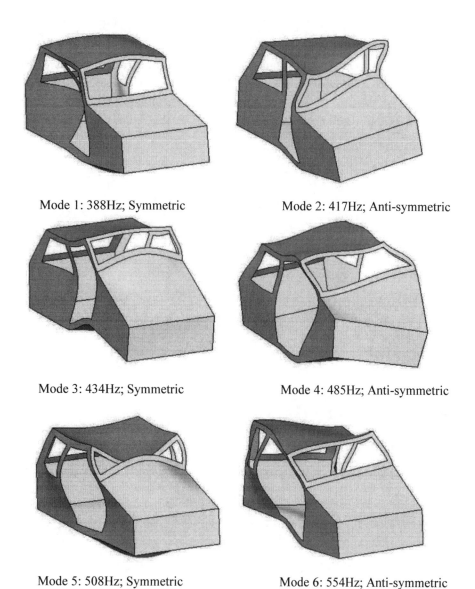

Mode 1: 388Hz; Symmetric   Mode 2: 417Hz; Anti-symmetric

Mode 3: 434Hz; Symmetric   Mode 4: 485Hz; Anti-symmetric

Mode 5: 508Hz; Symmetric   Mode 6: 554Hz; Anti-symmetric

Figure 7-4: Modal shapes and frequencies of the first six elastic modes.

It is a coincidence that the symmetric and anti-symmetric modes are alternating.

The property of a modal shape to be either symmetric or anti-symmetric applies to all structures with a plane of symmetry. You may want to return to the SHAFT model in chapter 6 to confirm this.

Having found this important property of vibration of symmetric structures, we may ask if analysis can be performed on one half of the model. If so, what boundary conditions should be defined? We will investigate this using the CAR model in the *02 half* configuration. We will first run a modal analysis with symmetry boundary conditions, then a modal analysis with anti-symmetry boundary conditions.

Switch to configuration *02 half*, create a **Frequency** study titled *02 sym*, exclude **Solid Body** from the analysis and define the same shell element thickness as before (50mm). Define **Symmetry Boundary Conditions** as shown in Figure 7-5.

Figure 7-5: Symmetry boundary conditions applied to the edges of the shell element model.

Symmetry boundary conditions leave the model with 3 Rigid Body Motions.

Symmetry boundary conditions must be defined in terms of six degrees of freedom: three translations and three rotations. This is because the model uses shell elements which have six degrees of freedom per node.

Symmetry boundary conditions do not restrain the model fully; it can translate in X and Y directions and can rotate about Z direction. Therefore, the first three modes will be **Rigid Body Modes**. To find the first six elastic modes, request 9 modes in the properties of study *02 sym*.

Obtain the solution of the *02 sym* study and copy it into a new study titled *03 anti-sym*. The *03 anti-sym* study uses anti-symmetry boundary conditions which are easy to define by editing the symmetry boundary conditions. The editing is just a "flip": degrees of freedom that were free in symmetry boundary conditions are restrained in anti-symmetry boundary conditions and vice-versa. Symmetry and anti-symmetry boundary conditions applied to edges in the plane of symmetry are shown in Figure 7-6.

Symmetry BC   Anti-Symmetry BC

Figure 7-6: Symmetry and anti-symmetry boundary conditions defined using the Front plane as reference geometry. Arrows indicate restrained directions.

The symmetry boundary condition window is a repetition of Figure 7-5.

The anti-symmetry boundary conditions do not fully restrain the model either. A summary of symmetry and anti-symmetry boundary conditions is shown in Figure 7-7.

	Symmetry BC	Anti-symmetry BC
X translation	Free	Fixed
Y translation	Free	Fixed
Z translation	Fixed	Free
X rotation	Fixed	Free
Y rotation	Fixed	Free
Z rotation	Free	Fixed

Figure 7-7: Summary of Rigid Body Motions in a model with symmetry and anti-symmetry boundary conditions.

Notice that what is fixed in symmetry boundary conditions is free in anti-symmetry boundary conditions and vice versa.

Obtain the solution of *03 anti-sym* and proceed to review of results of both studies. Animate the first three modes in study *02 sym* and in study *03 anti-sym* and confirm that they are **Rigid Body Modes** corresponding to rigid body displacements identified in Figure 7-7.

Animate the elastic modes found in study *02 sym*, these are Modes 4-9, and notice that all shapes are symmetric. Next, animate Modes 4-9 found in study *03 anti-sym* and notice that all shapes are anti-symmetric.

Symmetry boundary conditions eliminate anti-symmetric modes and anti-symmetry boundary conditions eliminate symmetric modes. Performing modal analysis on one half of the model first with symmetry boundary conditions then with anti-symmetry boundary conditions is called the **Modal Separation** technique.

One half of a symmetric model can be used to extract all modes of vibration by combining results of a modal analysis with symmetry boundary conditions with the results of modal analysis of the same model with anti-symmetry boundary conditions as it is schematically shown in Figure 7-8.

Study name		01 full		02 sym		03 anti-sym	
				All modes are symmetric		All modes are anti-symmetric	
	Mode No.	Hz		Mode No.	Hz		Mode No.	Hz
	1	0		1	0		1	0
	2	0		2	0		2	0
	3	0		3	0		3	0
	4	0		4	62		4	65
	5	0		5	68		5	76
	6	0		6	81		6	87
sym	7	62		7	88		7	91
anti-sym	8	66		8	96		8	145
sym	9	69		9	117		9	164
anti-sym	10	77						
sym	11	81						
anti-sym	12	88						

Figure 7-8: Summary of results of studies *01 full, 02 sym*, and *03 anti-sym.*

Borders around the first six modes of the unsupported full model (study 01 full) and around the first three modes of the partially supported models (studies 02 sym and 03 anti-sym) indicate Rigid Body Modes.

The solutions of study *01 full* may be obtained by merging solutions of study *02 sym* obtained with symmetry boundary conditions and *03 anti-sym* obtained with anti-symmetry boundary conditions.

The **Modal Separation** technique may also be used to directly find the first torsional mode, which is the first elastic mode in the model with anti-symmetry boundary conditions.

Summary of studies completed

Model	Configuration	Study Name	Study Type
CAR.sldprt	*01 full*	*01 full*	Frequency
	02 half	*02 sym*	Frequency
		03 anti-sym	Frequency

Figure 7-9: Names and types of studies completed in this chapter.

8: Modal analysis of axi-symmetric structures

Topics covered

- ❑ Modes of vibration of axi-symmetric structures
- ❑ Repetitive modes
- ❑ Solid and shell element modeling

The analysis of the SHAFT model in Chapter 6 and the CAR model in Chapter 7 revealed important properties of modal shapes of symmetric models and axially symmetric models. In this chapter we continue with the analysis of an axi-symmetric model. The model VASE comes in two configurations *01 solid* and *02 shell*. The wall thickness in *01 solid* is 2mm. The surface in *02 shell* has been offset 1mm into the material. Either configuration may be used for analysis of modes of vibration of this axi-symmetric model. We will use *02 shell* which is intended for meshing with shell elements. If you use *01 solid*, make sure to use a sufficiently small element size to avoid excessive element distortion. Your results will be slightly different because of the different modeling approach and different discretization error.

Configuration *01 solid*
Solid body intended for meshing
with solid elements

Configuration *02 shell*
Surface body intended for meshing
with shell elements

Figure 8-1: VASE model in two configurations.

Either configuration may be used for modal analysis.

Make sure the model is in the *02 shell* configuration and create a **Frequency** study titled *01 modal*. Verify that the material, **Ceramic Porcelain**, has been transferred from the CAD model.

You don't have to exclude the **SolidBody** because it has been deleted from the model in 02 shell configuration.

Define the shell thickness as 2mm (Figure 8-2).

(1)
Right-click
Surface folder
Select Edit
Definition

(2)
Select Thin
definition
Enter 2mm

(3)
Select
Middle
Surface

Figure 8-2: Thickness defined for Surface Body.

Middle Surface returns symmetric placement of thickness on both sides of the surface.

Define a **Fixed** restraint to the bottom of the VASE as shown in Figure 8-3.

Figure 8-3: Fixed restraint applied to the bottom face.

This restraint fully restrains the model but also eliminates any vibration of the bottom face. Restraints symbols are not shown.

Mesh the VASE model with the default element size and obtain solution for 12 modes. Vibration shapes and frequencies of the first two modes are shown in Figure 8-4.

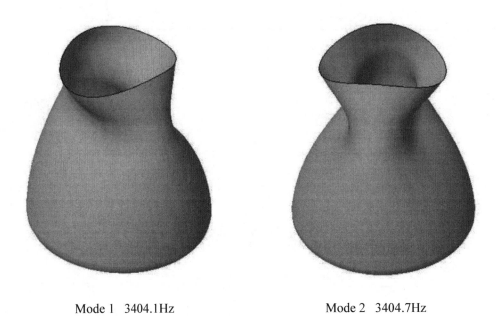

Mode 1   3404.1Hz   Mode 2   3404.7Hz

Figure 8-4: The first two modes of vibration.

The shape of both modes is identical but rotated about the axis of symmetry.

Repetitive modes characterize modal analysis results of axi-symmetric structures. The only reason these two modes do not have the same frequency is because of numerical error. The shape is also identical but rotated about the axis of symmetry. Theoretically, shapes of repetitive modes should be rotated by 90°. In the case of the VASE, the angle of rotation is lower because of numerical error. More repetitive modes are listed in Figure 8-5.

Mode number	Frequency Hz	
1	3404.1	Repetitive
2	3404.7	
3	4376.9	Repetitive
4	4378.4	
5	7931.2	Repetitive
6	7933.6	
7	8700.0	Axial mode
8	10835	Repetitive
9	10836	

Figure 8-5: The first nine frequencies of VASE. Repetitive modes are indicated.

Numerical error makes frequencies of each pair of repetitive modes slightly different.

Review results in Figure 8-5 and notice that the only non-repetitive mode is mode 7; this mode is associated with motion in the axial direction.

Summary of studies completed

Model	Configuration	Study Name	Study Type
VASE.sldprt	*02 shell*	*01 modal*	Frequency

Figure 8-6: Names and types of studies completed in this chapter.

9: Modal analysis – locating structurally weak spots

Topics covered

- ❑ Modal analysis with beam elements
- ❑ Modes of vibration of symmetric structures
- ❑ Using results of modal analysis to identify potential design problems
- ❑ Frequency shift

Procedure

Open the BAJA FRAME part (Figure 9-1). This model is an early iteration of a tubular frame designed by students of Western Engineering for the SAE BAJA competition. At an early stage of the design process, loads and restraints are largely unknown. Since modal analysis may be run without any restraints, an insight offered by modal analysis into structural properties of this design is particularly valuable.

Review the BAJA FRAME model and notice that all trims of Structural Members have been suppressed. Nodes are constructed in such a way that the center lines of the tubes all meet in one point. This was done to facilitate meshing with beam elements; manufacturing considerations will later require modifications to this design.

Figure 9-1: An early design iteration of Western Engineering's SAE BAJA frame.

The SOLIDWORKS model uses structural members suitable for meshing with beam elements.

We will use modal analysis to review how stiffness is distributed in the model and to locate potential "weak spots" of this space frame. This can be done without defining any restraints. Create a **Frequency** study titled *Study 1* and specify 12 modes in the study properties; remember that the first six modes will be RBMs. The frame is symmetric, except for two diagonal members in the back; the modes will be very close to symmetric and anti-symmetric.

Obtain the solution and animate the first two elastic modes. Considering that in the absence of restraints, the model has six Rigid Body Modes, the first two elastic modes will be mode 7 and mode 8. Figure 8-2 shows these two modes using displacement plots. The use of colors (invisible in this black and white illustration) makes it easy to locate areas with the largest displacements. While absolute displacements results are meaningless in modal analysis, relative displacements are valid; just remember to compare displacements only within the same mode. Comparing displacement results between different modes is a severe error of the interpretation of modal analysis results.

Mode 1
Bending 36Hz

Mode 1
Torsion 43Hz

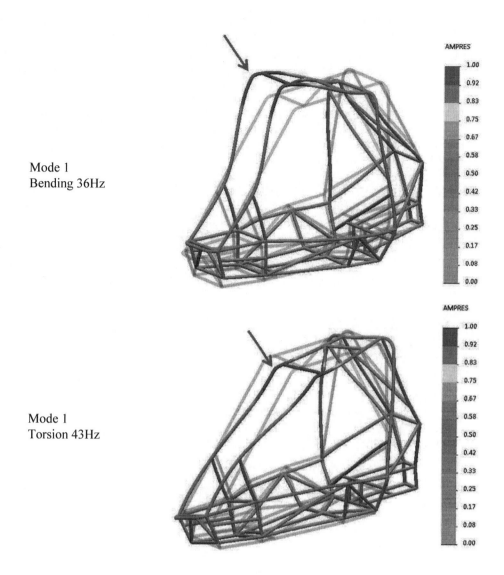

Figure 9-2: The first two elastic modes of vibration. Arrows locate areas with large displacements. In both modes this is the same location.

The undeformed shape is superimposed on displacement results. Numerical displacement results are normalized; they may be used for finding relative displacements within the same mode.

The first mode is a bending mode; the second mode is a torsional mode. Review all results to see which "weak spots" are highlighted by higher modes.

Numerical values of modal frequencies are of little use except to find out which portions of the frame are "soft." Notice that the BAJA FRAME will be stiffened by installing the engine, transmission, suspension, steering and driver's seat. At the same time these components will also add mass. Therefore, at this point the modal analysis provides only qualitative results.

Based on these qualitative results, Western Engineering SAE BAJA team decided to reinforce locations indicated in Figure 9-2. The redesign was important for the driver's safety because these locations are critically important in the case of a roll-over.

We'll use the BAJA FRAME model to introduce **Frequency Shift**. This solver option allows for calculating frequencies clustered around the specified frequency value. It may be used to eliminate calculation of 0Hz frequencies in models where **Rigid Body Modes** are present.

Copy the completed study into two more studies: *Study 2* and *Study 3,* and try out the **Frequency Shift** option using the settings shown in Figure 9-3 and Figure 9-4.

Properties of *Study 2*

Results of *Study 2:* One mode with frequency closest to 45Hz has been found

Figure 9-3: Properties and results of *Study 2* with one mode requested and frequency shift 45Hz.

Direct sparse solver must be used when Frequency Shift is requested.

Figure 9-4: Properties and results of *Study 3* with three modes requested and frequency shift 45Hz.

Direct sparse solver must be used when Frequency Shift is requested.

A **Frequency Shift** of 45Hz with just one mode requested finds the closest mode (43.2Hz) which is the torsional mode (Figure 9-3). A **Frequency Shift** with three modes requested finds modes 36.0Hz, 43.2Hz, and 54.3Hz (Figure 9-4). In both cases all rigid body modes are eliminated from the solution.

Summary of studies completed

Model	Configuration	Study Name	Study Type
BAJA FRAME.sldprt	*Default*	*Study 1*	Frequency
		Study 2	Frequency
		Study 3	Frequency

Figure 9-5: Names and types of studies completed in this chapter.

10: Modal analysis - a diagnostic tool

Topics covered

❏ Modal analysis used to detect problems with restraints
❏ Modal analysis used to detect connectivity problems
❏ Rigid Body Motion of assemblies

The ability of modal analysis to detect Rigid Body Motions can be used to diagnose modeling problems such as insufficient restraints or disconnected parts. If static analysis fails with the "insufficient restraints" or similar error message, you may still run a modal analysis on the same model and identify the direction(s) of movement corresponding to the 0Hz mode(s). This will identify the direction(s) where restraints are missing.

Procedure

The objective of the analysis of the PLIERS assembly is to find stresses in the arms of the pliers squeezing a plate as shown in Figure 10-1.

20 lbf

20 lbf

Fixed restraint
to the end face

Figure 10-1: A plate being held by pliers is modeled in the PLIERS assembly.

The arms are loaded with a normal force of 20lbf applied to split faces as shown. Two arms of the pliers are connected with a pin connector; the pin connector is hidden in this illustration.

Open the assembly model PLIERS; make sure it is in *01 error* configuration. The assembly model has a static study *01static* and frequency studies *02 modal* and *03 modal* defined. The two arms are connected with a pin connector and loaded with 20lbf each; the plate has a fixed support applied to one side face (Figure 10-1).

An attempt to solve **Static** study *01 static* produces an error message as shown in Figure 10-2.

Select No
to display
the lower window

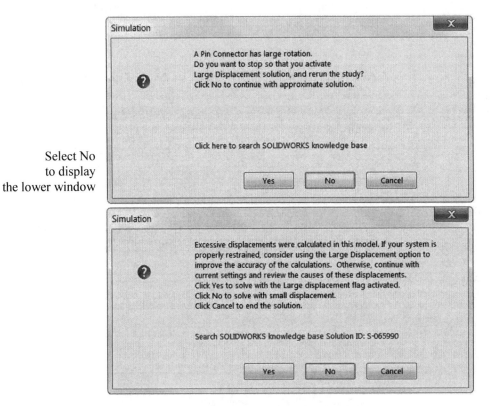

Figure 10-2: Error message issued by solver due to Rigid Body Motion detected in the model.

If you select No in the top window, the bottom window will be displayed.

The lack of "adequate fixtures" reported by both solvers is related to the presence of **Rigid Body Motions** (RBM) in the model; we will use modal analysis to find them. Knowing **the Rigid Body Motions** will help us identify problems with restraints.

Move to **Frequency** study titled *02 modal;* it has the same **Fixtures** and **Connectors** as the failed study *01 static*. There is no load in *02 modal* study.

At this point we know that there are unintentional RBMs in the model but we don't know how many are there; define the number of frequencies in study *02 modal* as 12. Select Use **FFEPlus** solver, obtain the solution and create **Frequency vs. Mode Number** graph to identify the RBMs in the model (Figure 10-3).

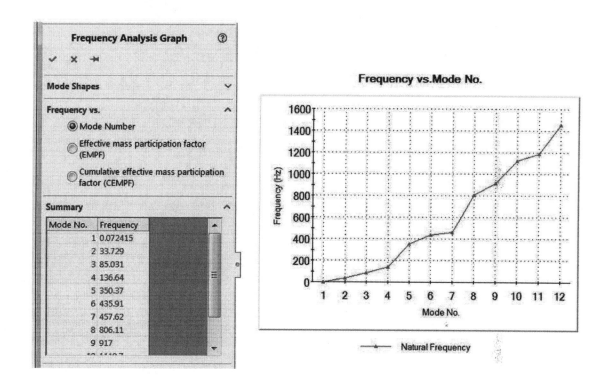

Figure 10-3: Mode 1 has near zero frequency.

There is one RBM in the model; the frequency of the first mode is not exactly zero because of discretization error.

Animation of the first mode reveals that one arm is able to rotate without any deformation.

This arm rotates as a rigid body

Figure 10-4: Deformed plots of mode 1; the plot may show the rotating arm in the opposite extreme position.

Animate this shape with undeformed model superimposed on displacement plots.

Animation of the mode of vibration corresponding to the **Rigid Body Mode** demonstrate that the moving arm is disconnected from the flat plate. Review the model to find small gaps between the jaw and the plate. This is the cause of "insufficient restraints" in the model.

The first mode where deformation is present is mode 2, shown in Figure 10-5.

Figure 10-5: Deformed plot of mode 2.

The flat plate deforms as a cantilever beam.

You may want to switch to the *02 correct* assembly configuration and repeat the modal analysis (study *03 modal*). This configuration uses a thicker flat plate which touches both jaws. The touching faces are bonded by the automesher and the FEA model behaves as one solid body avoiding the problem of missing connectivity.

The problems with the PLIERS assembly have been identified using modal analysis which worked as a tool to detect RBMs. This in turn led us to the problem of disconnected faces. An alternative approach would be to use a **Static** study with the option **Use soft springs to stabilize model** selected.

The second example of using modal analysis as a diagnostic tool will be run on incorrectly supported model.

Open the part FLAT, which belongs to PLIERS assembly. We'll use it to demonstrate an application of modal analysis to identify a problem with restraints. The model comes with two studies defined: *01 static* and *02 modal*, both ready to run. An attempt to run *01 static* study produces error message shown in Figure 10-6.

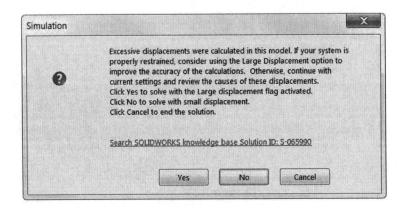

Figure 10-6: Solver error message in study *01 static*.

Error message identifies a problem with excessive displacements.

Selecting **Yes** fails the solution; selecting **No** produces clearly incorrect results with very large displacements.

The solution of study *02 modal* completes without an error message if FFEPlus solver is used. The **List Modes** table shows the first mode with a frequency of 0Hz (Figure 10-7).

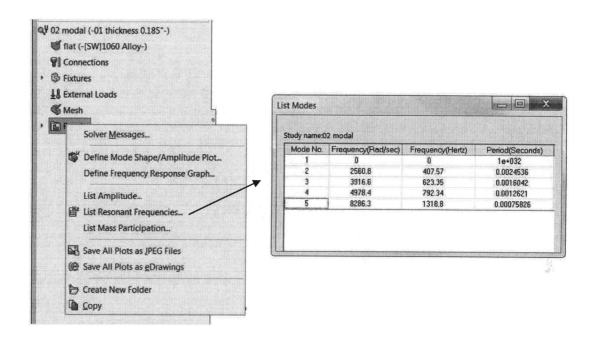

Figure 10-7: Results of *02 modal* study on part FLAT.

Mode 1 is a Rigid Body Mode with frequency 0Hz.

The modal frequencies may be listed by defining **Frequency Analysis Graph** (Figure 10-3) or using **List Resonant Frequencies** (Figure 10-7).

Animation of Mode 1 reveals the problem: the restraint is not fixed, even though it is called **Fixed**. The model has one RBM which is rotated about the edge where the **Fixed** restraint has been defined (Figure 10-8).

Deformed model

Undeformed model

The edge where **Fixed** restraint is defined becomes the axis of rotation

Figure 10-8: Result of modal analysis of FLAT part. Shape of Mode 1 which is a Rigid Body Mode.

Even though we use the terms "Undeformed model" and "Deformed model," there is no deformation at all present in the model. The model rotates about the edge line where the Fixed restraints are defined.

The reason why an RBM is present in the model where the **Fixed** restraint has been applied is that solid elements have three degrees of freedom per node and these are all translations. Consequently nodes of solid elements can't generate a moment reaction necessary to support the model and the model rotates about the line of support.

These are two simple examples of using modal analysis as a diagnostic tool. Both are based on the ability of modal analysis to identify rigid body motions which can't be identified in a structural analysis which will not run with motions.

You may have noticed that we alternate between two terms: **Rigid Body Motion** and **Rigid Body Mode**. The **Rigid Body Motion** is a displacement without any deformation. The **Rigid Body Mode** is the way of identifying **Rigid Body Motion** by modal analysis which assigns to it frequency 0Hz.

Summary of studies completed

Model	Configuration	Study Name	Study Type
PLIERS.sldasm	*01 error*	*01 static*	Static
		02 modal	Frequency
	02 correct	*03 modal*	Frequency
FLAT.sldprt	*01 thickness 0.185"*	*01 static*	Static
		02 modal	Frequency

Figure 10-9: Names and types of studies completed in this chapter.

11: Time response and frequency response of discrete systems

Topics covered

- Time response
- Steady state harmonic response
- Frequency sweep
- Displacement base excitation
- Velocity base excitation
- Acceleration base excitation
- Resonance
- Modal damping

In the previous chapters, we studied different applications of modal analysis which investigated structures' propensity to vibrate but that was not a vibration analysis. In chapter 1 we introduced the **Modal Superposition Method** which is a ubiquitous tool in Vibration Analysis. We'll be using it in all linear vibration problems.

Here is a short review of the **Modal Superposition Method**:

Modal Superposition Method

The **Modal Superposition Method** (MSM) represents a vibration response of a structure by using the superposition of responses that characterize Single Degree Of Freedom (SDOF) systems. The natural frequencies and directions of vibration of these SDOF systems correspond to the natural frequencies of the analyzed structure. The number of SDOFs contributing to a dynamic response is equal to the number of modes calculated by a pre-requisite modal (frequency) analysis.

How many modes should be calculated to represent a vibration response using the MSM? The first few modes are the most important, but the exact number of required modes is not known prior to analysis. Ideally, one should use a convergence process to demonstrate that increasing the number of modes past a certain number no longer significantly affects results.

Vibration analysis based on the MSM may be categorized into two major types: **Time Response** analysis and **Frequency Response** analysis. **Time Response** analysis is called **Modal Time History** in **SOLIDWORKS Simulation**; a **Frequency Response** analysis is called **Harmonic**. We'll be alternating between these terms just like we alternate between the terms **Modal** analysis and **Frequency** analysis.

Time Response (Modal Time History) analysis

In a **Time Response** analysis, the applied load is an explicit function of time. Damping is taken into consideration and the vibration equation appears in its full form:

$$[M]\ddot{d} + [C]\dot{d} + [K]d = F(t)$$

Where:

[M]	mass matrix
[C]	damping matrix
[K]	stiffness matrix
F(t)	vector of nodal loads (this vector is a function of time)
d	unknown vector of nodal displacements

A **Time Response** analysis requires the definition of a damping coefficient which is most often expressed as a percentage of critical damping. Readers are referred to (9) listed in Chapter 21 for numerical values of damping coefficients.

A **Time Response** analysis is used to model events of a short duration. A typical example would be an analysis of a structure's vibrations due to an impact load or acceleration applied to the base (called base excitation). Results of the **Time Response** analysis capture both the transient response and steady state vibration response.

Frequency Response (Harmonic) analysis

A **Harmonic** analysis assumes that the load is a function of frequency rather than being directly dependent on time as is the case of a **Time Response** analysis.

$$[M]\ddot{d} + [C]\dot{d} + [K]d = F(Asin(\omega t) + Bcos(\omega t))$$

Where:

[M]	mass matrix
[C]	damping matrix
[K]	stiffness matrix
F(t)	vector of nodal loads (this vector is a function of frequency)
d	unknown vector of nodal displacements

A **Frequency Response** analysis models a structure's response to a forced excitation or base excitation (excitation applied to its supports) that is a harmonic function of time. It is assumed that the excitation frequency changes very slowly, hence the alternative name **Steady State Harmonic Response** is often used for this type of analysis. A **Frequency Response** analysis also uses the modal superposition method and requires that damping be defined, usually as a percentage of critical damping.

A typical application of a **Frequency Response** analysis is a simulation of a shaker table test discussed in Chapter 12.

In this chapter we introduce both **Time Response** and **Frequency Response** analyses using a simple discrete vibrating system. Open assembly model MDOF and review the three configurations *1DOF, 2DOF, and 3DOF* as shown in Figure 11-1. The same figure shows sensor locations in each configuration.

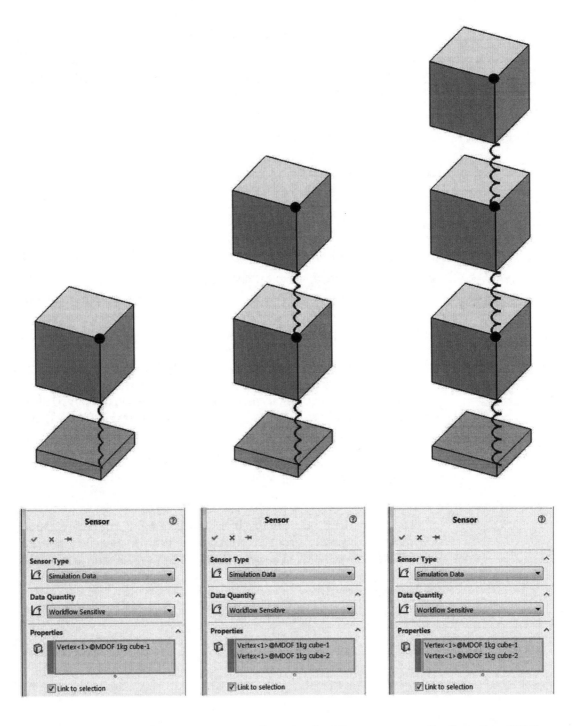

Configuration *1DOF*   Configuration *2DOF*   Configuration *3DOF*

Figure 11-1: Assembly model MDOF in three configurations; all cubes are identical; arrows indicate sensor locations.

Verify that the mass of each cube is 1kg. Black dots indicate sensor locations.

Cubes are connected by linear springs. The stiffness of each spring is 10000N/m. Each cube may move only in the vertical direction (Figure 11-2).

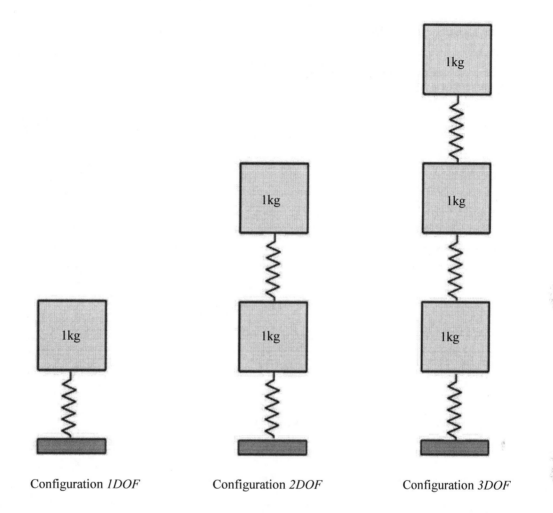

Configuration *1DOF*   Configuration *2DOF*   Configuration *3DOF*

Figure 11-2: Assembly components are connected with linear springs.

All springs in all configurations have the same stiffness: 10000N/m.

We'll use the *MDOF* assembly to run as many as ten studies. Because of this complexity we present the summary now rather than at the end of the chapter.

Summary of studies

All configurations and all studies are in the same assembly model MDOF.sldasm.

Configuration	Study name	Study type	Description
1DOF	*01 1DOF modal*	Frequency	Modal analysis
2DOF	*02 2DOF modal*	Frequency	Modal analysis
3DOF	*03 3DOF modal*	Frequency	Modal analysis
1DOF	*04 1DOF disp fr*	Linear Dynamic Harmonic	Frequency Response analysis with displacement base excitation
1DOF	*05 1DOF vel fr*	Linear Dynamic Harmonic	Frequency Response analysis with velocity base excitation
1DOF	*06 1DOF acc fr*	Linear Dynamic Harmonic	Frequency Response analysis with acceleration base excitation
2DOF	*07 2DOF disp fr*	Linear Dynamic Harmonic	Frequency Response analysis with displacement base excitation
3DOF	*08 3DOF disp fr*	Linear Dynamic Harmonic	Frequency Response analysis with displacement base excitation
1DOF	*09 1DOF shock tr*	Linear Dynamic Modal Time History	Time Response analysis with shock load
1DOF	*10 1DOF initial cond tr*	Linear Dynamic Modal Time History	Time Response analysis with initial condition

Figure 11-3: MDOF assembly configurations and studies discussed in this chapter.

We'll now discuss restraints, spring connectors and meshing which are common to all configurations and all studies.

All cubes have **Roller/Slider** restraints defined to all side faces (Figure 11-4).

Figure 11-4: Roller/Slider restraints applied to four sides of each cube shown here for configuration *1DOF*.

Roller/Slider restraints may be applied only to two perpendicular faces; this will be sufficient to limit the motion to the vertical direction only.

Symbol of Spring Connector is shown; symbols of restraints applied to the base are not shown.

The base part has **Fixed** restraints applied, they may be applied to one face, to selected faces or to all faces.

All springs are modeled as spring connectors (Figure 11-5).

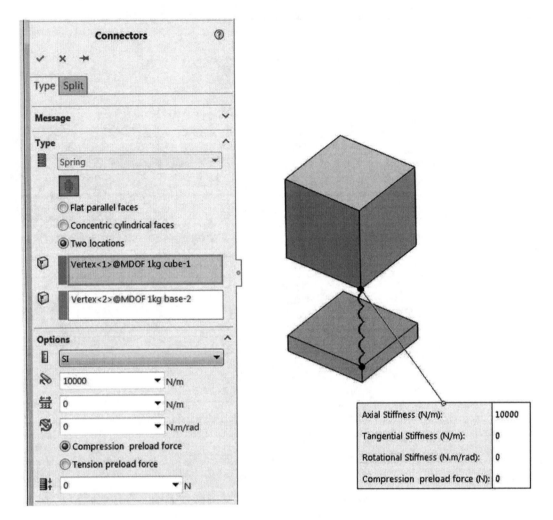

Figure 11-5: Spring connector shown for the model in configuration *1DOF*.
10000N/m is the linear stiffness.

We are modeling discrete systems. In these systems stiffness properties are fully defined by the springs and inertial properties are defined by the cubes. As we'll soon demonstrate, the cubes do not deform in these modes which are of interest to us. Therefore, the cubes and base may be meshed with a coarse mesh; use element size 20mm in all configurations.

Run **Frequency** studies on configurations *01 1DOF modal, 02 2DOF modal*, and *03 3DOF modal* to find the modes of vibration. You will find that the number of modes that are associated with the deformation of the springs corresponds to the number of degrees of freedom in each configuration. Remember, when we say "the number of degrees of freedom" we are referring to all the solid elements (cubes and base) as rigid bodies.

Results of modal analyses are summarized in Figure 11-6.

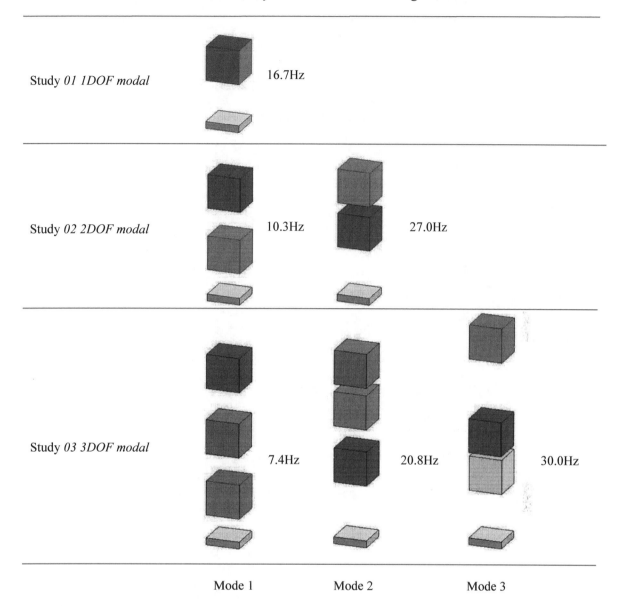

Figure 11-6: Summary of the results of modal analysis in all assembly configurations.

Configurations are arranged in rows; modes are arranged in columns.

You may want to review the shapes of higher modes to see that they are associated with deformation of cubes and do not correspond to the discrete system we analyze here.

Configuration 1DOF has an analytical solution $\omega = \sqrt{k/m} = 100$rad/s which is very close to the numerical solution f = 16.7Hz ($\omega = 2\Pi$f).

From the results of the modal analysis presented in Figure 11-5, we learned that the range of frequencies, 0 – 30Hz, includes all natural frequencies of the system in all assembly configurations.

In the **Frequency Response** analysis that we are about to perform, we subject the base to oscillations with frequencies from zero (no motion) to frequencies much higher than the highest frequency. A frequency three times as high as the natural frequency is generally considered as a "much higher" frequency; therefore, the range of base excitation frequencies will be 0-90Hz. In the **Harmonic** analysis with base excitation, the base is subjected to harmonic motion as shown in Figure 11-7.

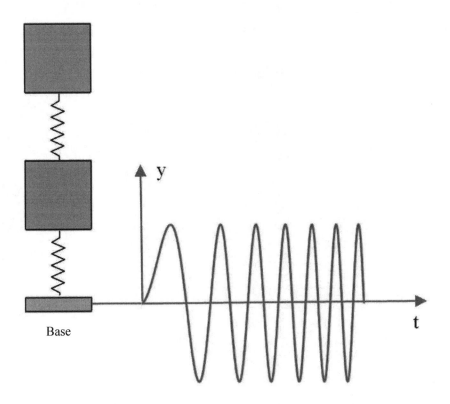

Figure 11-7: Harmonic base excitation applied to the base shown here for configuration *2DOF*.

The base performs harmonic motion with constant amplitude and increasing frequency.

Three different types of base excitation will be applied:

- Excitation with constant displacement amplitude
- Excitation with constant velocity amplitude
- Excitation with constant acceleration amplitude

Start in the *1 DOF* assembly configuration and create a **Harmonic** study titled *04 1DOF disp fr* as shown in Figure 11-8. This is the first study in the series of three **Harmonic** studies: *04 1DOF disp fr, 05 1DOF vel fr,* and *06 1DOF acc fr.*

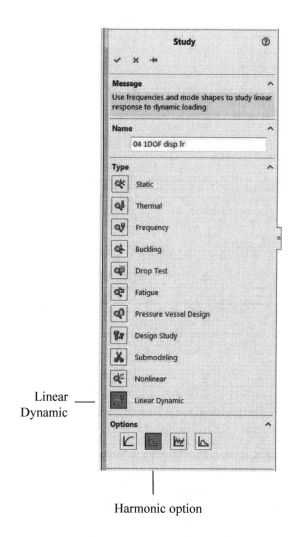

Linear Dynamic

Harmonic option

Figure 11-8: Definition of a Harmonic study.

Harmonic study is one of four options in Linear Dynamic study.

Harmonic analysis is also called Frequency Response analysis.

Define study properties as shown in Figure 11-9.

Frequency Options   Harmonic Options

Figure 11-9: Definition of the Harmonic study.

The definition consists of specifying Frequency Options and Harmonic Options.

Like all **Linear Dynamic** studies, the **Harmonic** study is based on the **Modal Superposition Method**. The **Number of frequencies** specified in **Frequency Options** gives the number of modes to be used to find the vibration response. In this exercise we analyze a discrete vibration system with one degree of freedom which had one mode of vibration. For this reason the **Number of frequencies** is 1. The **Operating frequency limits** defined in **Harmonic Options** specifies the range of frequencies to which the model will be subjected. The vibration response will be found as function of the excitation frequency slowly changing from 0 to 90Hz.

Define a **Fixed** restraint to base and **Roller/Slider** restraints the same as in the previously completed **Frequency** analyses.

Define **Base Excitation** as shown in Figure 11-10.

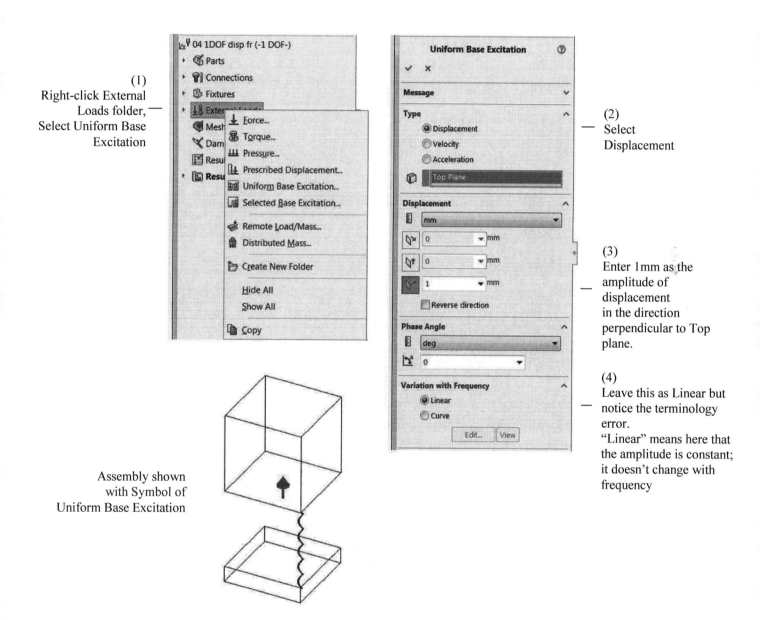

(1)
Right-click External Loads folder, — Select Uniform Base Excitation

(2)
— Select Displacement

(3)
— Enter 1mm as the amplitude of displacement in the direction perpendicular to Top plane.

(4)
— Leave this as Linear but notice the terminology error.
"Linear" means here that the amplitude is constant; it doesn't change with frequency

Assembly shown with Symbol of Uniform Base Excitation

Figure 11-10: Definition of Uniform Base Excitation.

The wireframe display is used to clearly show the symbol of Uniform Base Excitation. The symbols of the Roller/Slider restraints applied to all four sides of the cube and symbols for the Fixed restraints applied to all faces of the base are not shown in this illustration.

Uniform Base Excitation means that the base excitation is applied through all restraints active in the specified direction. In our case it means that it is applied to the base but not to the cube, because the cube does not have any restraints in the direction of excitation. **Variation with Frequency** is defined as **Linear** but this should say **Constant**; the amplitude doesn't change with the excitation frequency.

Apply **Modal Damping** as shown in Figure 11-11.

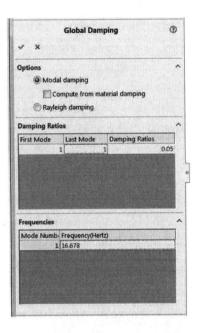

Figure 11-11: A Modal Damping of 5% is defined for the only mode present in this discrete vibrating system.

Modal damping may be defined directly or may be computed from material damping. Here, we use the first method.

A **Modal damping** of 5% means that damping in the system equals 5% of critical damping. Oscillatory motion is not possible for critical damping or higher. This definition of damping doesn't specify which model component is responsible for dissipating energy. This is why the window in Figure 11-11 is called **Global Damping**.

Define **Results Options** as shown in Figure 11-12:

Figure 11-12: Result Options definition.

This window defines which steps will be used for creating Response Graphs. Here, all steps will be used. The number referring to the last step may be defined as higher than the actual number of preformed steps. Here, the end step is defined as step 1000 which is the highest number allowed by the system.

Obtain the solution and define a **Response Graph** as shown in Figure 11-13.

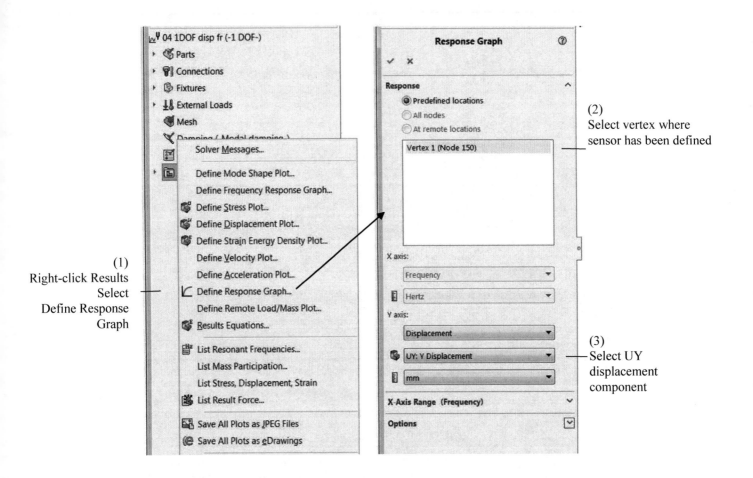

Figure 11-13: Response Graph definition.

Displacement component UY is in the direction of base excitation.

Before analyzing results of study *04 1DOF disp fr*, we'll define and run two more **Harmonic** studies, then we'll analyze all the results together. Copy study *04 1DOF disp fr* into *05 1DOF vel fr*, then copy it into *06 1DOF acc fr*. Edit the two new studies as shown in Figure 11-14; the only difference between these three studies is in the base excitation definition.

Study *04 1DOF disp fr*
Displacement excitation
amplitude 0.001m

Study *05 1DOF vel fr*
Velocity excitation
amplitude 0.1m/s

Study *06 1DOF acc fr*
Acceleration excitation
amplitude 10m/s²

Figure 11-14: Base excitation definition in three Harmonic studies with base excitation.

The left window is a repetition of Figure 11-10.

The results are summarized in Figure 11-15.

Study *04 1DOF disp fr*   Study *05 1DOF vel fr*   Study *06 1 DOF acc fr*

Figure 11-15: UY displacement amplitude as a function of the excitation frequency.

These graphs have been formatted in Excel.

UY displacement amplitude response graphs presented in Figure 11-15 all show one peak that corresponds to 16Hz (100rad/s) which is the natural frequency of the system in the *1DOF* configuration. For low damping, as is the case in this exercise, the amplitude of displacement reaches a maximum when the excitation frequency equals the natural frequency; this is called resonance.

Let's explain why in this exercise the displacement amplitude at resonance is the same for all three types of base excitation. Displacement, velocity, and acceleration in a harmonic motion are:

$$x = Asin(\omega t)$$

$$\dot{x} = A\omega cos(\omega t)$$

$$\ddot{x} = -A\omega^2 sin(\omega t)$$

Displacement amplitude is proportional to the base excitation, be it displacement, velocity, or acceleration excitation. Considering that $\omega = 100 rad/s$ is the frequency of excitation at resonance, the numerical value of acceleration amplitude is 100 times higher than the velocity amplitude and 10000 higher than displacement amplitude. Our definition of acceleration base excitation ($10m/s^2$), velocity base excitation (0.1m/s) and displacement base excitation (0.001m) follow the same ratio. Therefore, the displacement amplitude at resonance is the same for all three types of base excitation.

Examination of the response graphs in Figure 11-15 reveals an important property of displacement base excitation: the amplitude of vibration remains constant for frequencies much higher than the resonance.

We'll now conduct the analysis of the assembly in *2DOF* and *3DOF* configurations, limiting it to displacement base excitation with amplitude of 1mm and a frequency sweep of 0-90Hz. In the properties of study *07 2DOFdisp fr* define 2 modes, and in the properties of study *08 3DOF disp fr* define 3 modes in **Frequency Options**.

Define a **Base Excitation** as shown in Figure 11-10. Define **Modal Damping** for all modes present in each study. Spring connectors, restraints and the mesh remain the same.

Study *07 2DOFdisp fr* has two sensors; study *08 3DOFdisp fr* has three sensors; define **Results Options** for all sensors present in each study. Obtain solutions and define UY **Response Graphs**.

The frequency responses of UY displacement amplitude for all three studies are summarized in Figure 11-16.

Study *04 1DOF disp fr*   Study *07 2DOF disp fr*   Study *08 3DOF disp fr*

Figure 11-16: UY displacement amplitude as a function of the excitation frequency for the three assembly configurations.

The graph on the left has been already shown in Figure 11-14.

The number of peaks in these three frequency sweeps illustrated in Figure 11-15 equals the number of modes of vibration present in each study. The first mode dominates the displacement amplitude response in all cases. Please review the spreadsheet MDOF.xlsx for more details impossible to show in these black and white illustrations.

We now move to a **Time Response** analysis using the same *MDOF* assembly in configuration *1DOF*. Make sure the assembly is in *1DOF* configurations and create a study titled *09 1DOF shock tr* as shown in Figure 11-17.

Linear Dynamic

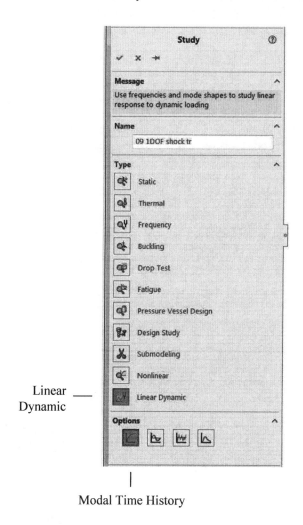

Modal Time History

Figure 11-17: Definition of a Time Response study called Modal Time History in SOLIDWORKS Simulation.

Modal Time History is one of four options in Linear Dynamic study. Modal Time History analysis is also called Time Response analysis.

A vibration response in a **Time Response** study is a function of time. In the study properties we must specify the time duration of the analysis and the time step. The duration of analysis will be 10 times the period of the mode of vibration with 10 time steps per oscillation. Remembering that the natural frequency is 100rad/s, the period of vibration is:

$$T = \frac{2\,\Pi}{\omega} = 0.063s$$

The duration of analysis is 0.63s and the time step 0.0063s. Define the properties of the **Modal Time History** study as shown in Figure 11-18.

Frequency Options   Dynamic Options

Figure 11-18: Properties of the Time response study.

Given time duration of 0.63s and a time step of 0.0063, the analysis will complete in 100 steps.

Use the same restraints, **Results Options**, and mesh size as in study *04 1DOF disp fr*.

Damping in a **Modal Time History** analysis may be defined in two different ways: as **Modal Damping**, the same as in a **Harmonic** study, or as linear damping in a **Spring-Damper** connector.

We'll work with the same 5% modal damping as before but we'll express it as linear damping in the definition of a **Spring-Damper** connector. The critical damping in a Single Degree of Freedom oscillator is:

$$c_{cr} = 2\sqrt{km} = 200\,\frac{Ns}{m} \qquad k = 10000\,\frac{N}{m} \quad m = 1kg$$

$$c = 0.05c_{cr} = 10\,\frac{Ns}{m}$$

Therefore, to define damping as 5% of critical damping we can either enter 10Ns/m in the **Spring-Damper Connector** window, or as 0.05 in the **Global Damping** window (Figure 11-19).

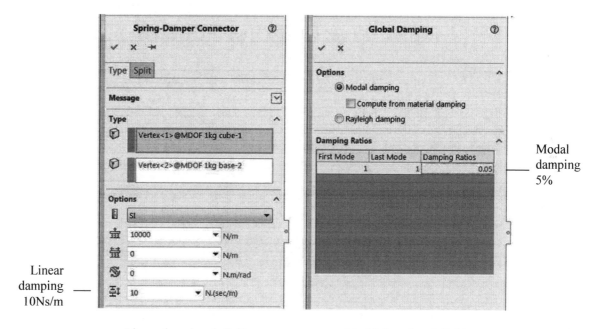

Linear damping 10Ns/m

Modal damping 5%

Linear damping definition   Modal damping definition

Figure 11-19: Damping can be defined explicitly as a linear damping (left) or as a fraction of critical damping (right). The entries in both windows define the same damping.

Define damping as a linear damping. If you define damping using both methods at the same time, the resultant damping will be 10% modal.

A **Time Response** analysis requires a load defined as a function of time. Here, we want to model the system response to a shock load, which is a load of short duration. In our example the load duration is 0.01s, the maximum load magnitude is 1000N, and the shape of the load time history curve is half a sine curve (Figure 11-20).

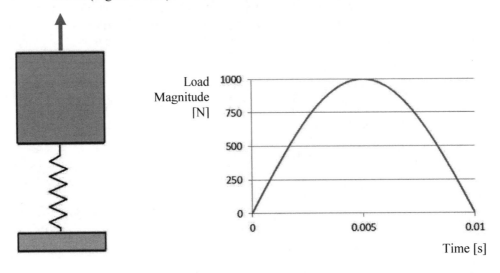

Figure 11-20: Shock load applied in the direction of motion of the 1DOF model.

Load is applied to the top face; it disappears after 0.01s.

To define this load, follow the steps in Figure 11-21.

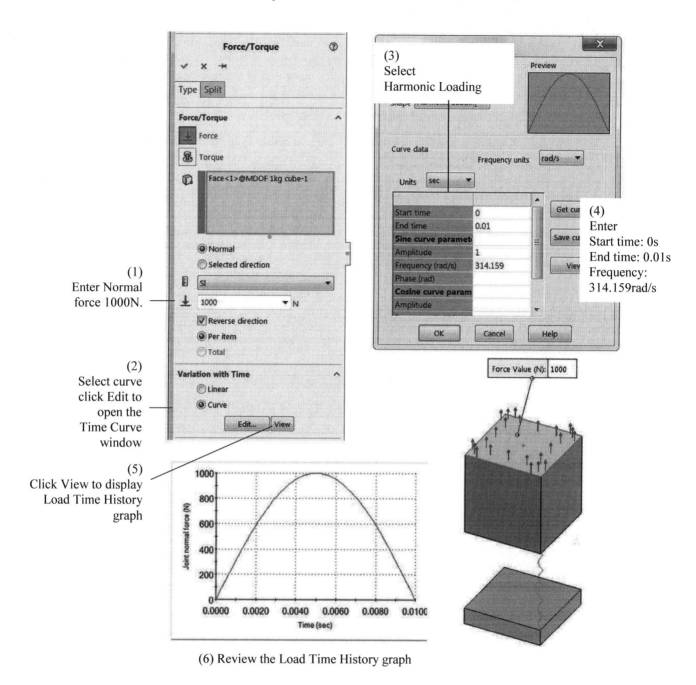

(6) Review the Load Time History graph

Figure 11-21: Defining load as a function of time. The force takes 0.005s to reach the maximum of 1000N, then another 0.005s to drop back to zero.

Select Variation with Time as Curve (2), and click Edit to open the Time curve definition window. Define the shape as harmonic loading (3) and enter values as shown (4). Click View (5) to examine the Load time history curve (6).

Notice that neither the entry in the **Force** window (here 1000N) nor the values defining the **Time curve** define the load time history on their own. The corresponding values are multiplied to calculate the force magnitude as a function of time.

Define **Results Options** as shown in Figure 11-12.

The duration of the load is 0.01s (Figure 11-20), while the duration of analysis is 0.63s (Figure 11-18) meaning that the load disappears after 0.01s and the system enters into free vibration. Run *09 1DOF tr shock* study and observe that it completes in 100 steps.

Right-click the *Results* folder and follow the steps illustrated in Figure 11-22 to create a graph showing displacement in the sensor location as a function of time.

<u>Figure 11-22: Displacement of the 1kg mass for the first 0.63s after load application.</u>

Notice that after 0.01s, excitation becomes zero and the mass performs free damped oscillations.

There is one more study left to run. Copy the last study *09 1DOF shock tr* into *10 1DOF initial cond tr*. These two studies are identical except for the method used to excite vibration. In study *09 1DOF shock tr* we used a load of very short duration and called it a Shock Load. This time dependent load acting over 0.01s generates an impulse load of 6.31Ns (Figure 11-23).

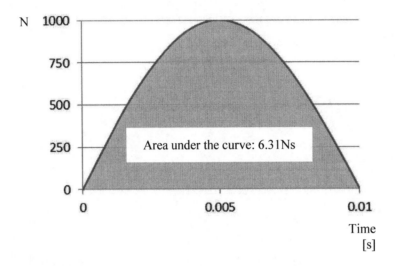

Figure 11-23: Impulse of the time dependent load is equal to the area under the curve.

See MDOF IMPULSE.xlsx.

Considering that:

$$mv_0 = Ft \qquad where \ m = 1kg \qquad Ft = 6.31Ns$$

we find the initial velocity of the 1kg mass that gives an equivalent excitation as the above time dependent load:

$$v_0 = \frac{Ft}{m} = 6.31 \frac{m}{s}$$

In study *10 1DOF initial cond tr* we set the system in motion by using an initial condition rather than a time dependent load.

Delete the load that was copied from study *09 1DOF shock tr* and define an initial condition as shown in Figure 11-24.

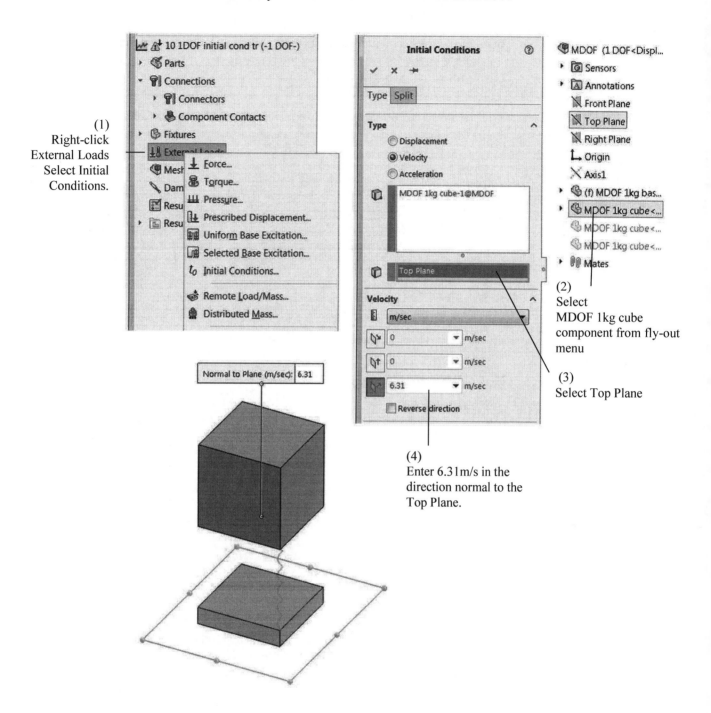

Figure 11-24: Definition of the initial condition.

The initial velocity definition applies to the entire cube assembly component.

Obtain the solution and review the UY displacement response graph and compare it with the same UY displacement response graph from the previous study. Both graphs are shown side by side in Figure 11-25.

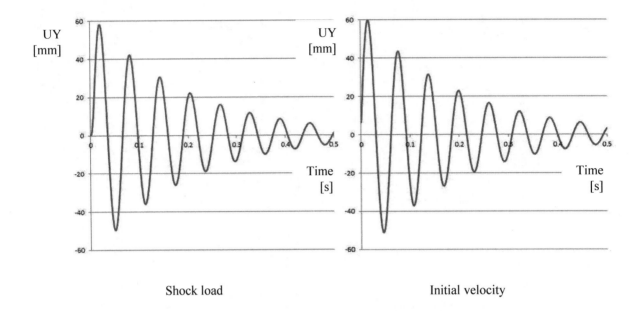

Shock load

Initial velocity

Figure 11-25: UY displacement response to the shock load and to the initial velocity.

Both graphs are identical except for the first 0.01s when the shock load is active.

Results shown in Figure 11-24 show that in a single degree of freedom system the effect of a shock load (load of a very short duration) may be modeled by an equivalent initial velocity.

You may want to extend this exercise even further and investigate the effect of different damping on the vibration response. This may be easily done using, for example, study *06 1DOF acc fr*. This study was run with a modal damping 5%. Re-run the same study with damping 2% and 10% and summarize the UY displacement responses in one graph as shown in Figure 11-26.

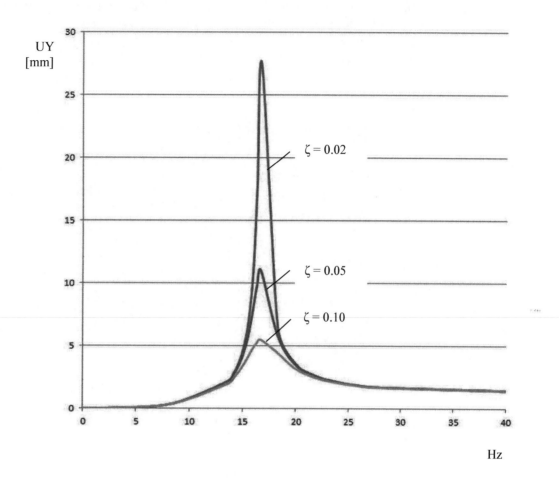

Figure 11-26: The amplitude of vibration as a function of excitation frequency for different modal damping values.

Damping strongly affects the amplitude for excitation frequencies close to the resonant frequency. It has no effect for excitation frequencies much lower or much higher than the resonant frequency.

Remember that the amplitude of vibration is always measured from the neutral position, not between negative and positive peaks.

As a side topic, not directly related to any of the analyses performed in this chapter, we'll point out the following. Since **Modal Time History** requires results of a **Frequency** analysis, a **Frequency** analysis is always run prior to a **Modal Time History**. Within **Modal Time History**, you may select to run only the **Frequency** analysis (Figure 11-27).

Figure 11-27: The pop-up menu invoked by right-clicking the Time Response study folder.

The Modal Time History study gives an option to run just the Frequency study without subsequent dynamic analyses.

Since a **Frequency** analysis is a part of **Modal Time History** and **Harmonic** studies, results of both these studies include the same results that are available in a **Frequency** study. To verify this, go back to the results of any **Modal Time History** or **Harmonic** studies and define a mode shape plot. You will see only as many frequencies as has been specified in the properties of the corresponding studies.

12: Harmonic base excitation of distributed systems

Topics covered

- Steady state harmonic excitation
- Frequency sweep
- Displacement base excitation
- Resonance
- Modal damping

This chapter partially repeats the topics related to harmonic base excitation introduced in Chapter 11 and expands it to analysis of vibration induced stresses in a distributed system.

Steady state harmonic excitation

The harmonic excitation may take the form of force/torque excitation or a base excitation where harmonic displacement, velocity, or acceleration is applied to the structure's restraints. Harmonic excitation is very common in engineering design problems. Rotating equipment may be subjected to harmonic excitation due to unbalanced loads, and many other types of excitations can be approximated successfully by harmonic excitation. In this chapter we'll model the vibration response of a structure subjected to harmonic base excitation where displacement of restraints is a sine function of time:

$$x = A sin(\omega t)$$

where:

A - displacement amplitude

ω - angular frequency

Harmonic base excitation may be realized experimentally by placing the tested structure on a shaker table which oscillates with displacement amplitude A and frequency ω (Figure 12-1).

Tested object
ELBOW PIPE

Shaker table

Fixed base

x

A

t

Figure 12-1: Schematic representation of a shaker table.

The shaker table oscillates relative to the base moving up and down with displacement amplitude A and frequency ω.

In the lower illustration cross-section view is used to show the base; the table is shown in the neutral (mid-stroke) position. The coordinate system is fixed to the base meaning that displacement is measured relative to the fixed base.

The model shown in Figure 12-1 is the SHAKER assembly. It is for show only and won't be analyzed; a component of this assembly, ELBOW PIPE, will be analyzed.

A shaker test is often conducted in such a way that the displacement amplitude remains constant while the frequency of excitation changes within a certain range. This is done to investigate the response of a tested object to excitation with different frequencies. The test is called a **Frequency Sweep** and will be simulated in this chapter by subjecting the part model ELBOW PIPE to base excitation in the frequency range of 0 - 400Hz.

Why should we use the frequency range of 0 - 400Hz? We assume that this is the range of excitation frequencies the part will see in service. A very important assumption has to be made: the rate of change of the excitation frequency is assumed to be very low. Therefore, the vibration response is a steady state response; transient response is not modeled. As we already know from Chapter 11, in **SOLIDWORKS Simulation** the analysis we need to conduct is called the **Linear Dynamic** study with a **Harmonic** option. Vibration analysis textbooks call this a **Steady State Harmonic Response**.

In preparation of the **Steady State Harmonic Response** analysis, we have to run two preparatory analyses.

First we'll run a static study to identify the location of stress concentrations and to design a mesh that will correctly model them. Using information from that static study we'll know where to locate stress sensors.

Next, we'll run a modal analysis to see how many modes of vibration are in the 0 - 400Hz frequency range. This way we'll know how many modes have to be considered in the vibration response analysis based on the **Modal Superposition Method**.

Open part model ELBOW PIPE and create a **Static** study *Gravity*. Apply a gravity load of 9.81m/s^2 as shown in Figure 12-2.

Figure 12-2: Load in the static study is the gravity load.

Gravity load 9.81m/s^2 is normal to the Top reference plane.

This load is not supposed to model real life loading conditions during the frequency sweep, but being a volume load is qualitatively close to the loading that the model will experience during the **Frequency Sweep**. We need it only to locate stress concentrations and to design the mesh. Absolute magnitudes of stress do not matter.

Apply restraints as shown in Figure 12-3; the same restraints will be used in all studies in this chapter.

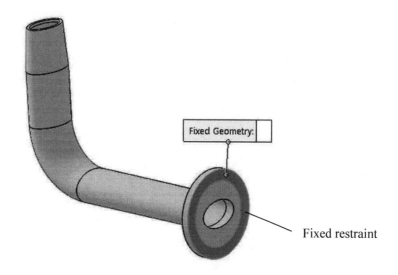

Figure 12-3: Restraints to the ELBOW PIPE model.

Apply a fixed restraint to the face created by the split line. This restraint approximates the attachment to another pipe with a flange of the same size.

Define a mesh control on the fillet near the flange as shown in Figure 12-4.

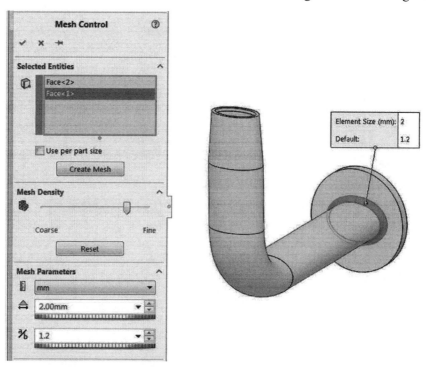

Figure 12-4: Mesh control to the fillet; notice that the fillet face is divided into two faces by a split line.

Use a 2mm element size on the controlled entity and the ratio of transition, a/b, equal to 1.2.

Having applied the mesh control, mesh the model with a global element size of 8mm and obtain the static solution. Review **P1 stress** results and confirm the location of the stress concentrations as shown in Figure 12-5. Remember that von Mises stress is not applicable to brittle material **Gray Cast Iron** which has been assigned to the model.

Location of the maximum P1 stress

Figure 12-5: Location of the highest P1 stress.

This location coincides with the split lines placed there to mark the location of a stress sensor.

Based on the results of this qualitative stress analysis, we define the first sensor in the location shown in Figure 12-5 and Figure 12-6; it will be used to create **Stress Response** graphs. Define the second sensor as shown in Figure 12-6; this one will be used to create **Displacement Response** graphs.

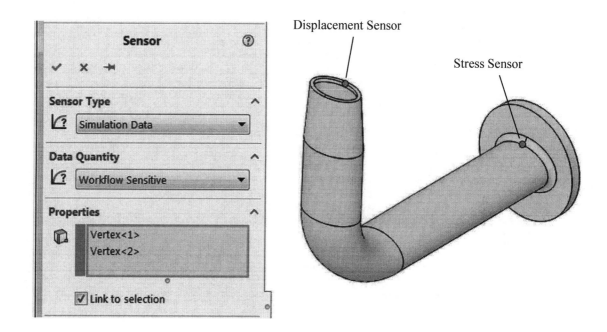

Figure 12-6: Sensor locations: two locations are defined in one Sensor window.

Both sensors use split lines in the model for defining their locations. These sensors are already defined in the SOLIDWORKS model.

Review once more the results of the *Gravity* study and notice that the highest P1 stress is not exactly in the **Stress Sensor** location and that a somewhat irregular shape of stress fringes (use Discrete Fringes) indicates that a more refined mesh is required. We'll use this sensor location for simplicity of its definition. We'll use a relatively coarse mesh to speed up the otherwise long solution time of the **Harmonic** studies. Once done, you are encouraged to repeat the analysis with a **Stress Sensor** located on the curved face using a more refined mesh.

Create a **Frequency** study titled *Modal* with properties shown in Figure 12-7.

Upper bound
frequency 400Hz

Figure 12-7: Properties of the frequency study; upper bound frequency of 400Hz selected.

Specifying an Upper bound frequency of 400Hz means that all modes in the frequency range of 0-400Hz will be found.

Obtain the modal solution and list the modes in the 0-400Hz range as shown in Figure 12-8. Remember that you may also run a modal analysis within the **Harmonic** study as explained in Chapter 11.

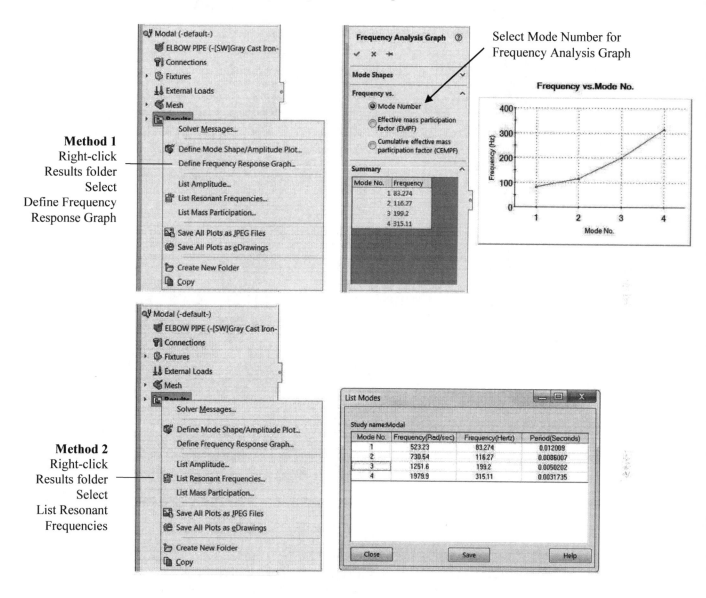

Method 1
Right-click
Results folder
Select
Define Frequency
Response Graph

Method 2
Right-click
Results folder
Select
List Resonant
Frequencies

Figure 12-8: Results of modal analysis show four modes within the range of 0-400Hz.

Two methods of showing results are demonstrated: as Frequency Response Graph (top) and as List Modes (bottom). List Modes window shows modal frequencies using three units: rad/s, Hz, s. The relation between frequency ω (rad/s) and f (Hz) is: ω =2Πf. The relation between frequency f (Hz) and period T(s) is: f=1/T.

Review modal shapes shown in Figure 12-9:

Deformed

Undeformed

Mode 1: 106Hz

Mode 2: 108Hz

Mode 3: 295Hz

Mode 4: 300Hz

<u>Figure 12-9: Modal shapes shown with the undeformed model superimposed on the deformed model.</u>

All modes are shown in the same view.

As shown in Figure 12-9, vibration in modes 1 and 3 take place in the XY plane; vibration in modes 2 and 4 takes place in YZ plane. The base excitation is applied in the Y direction; therefore only mode 1 and mode 3 will be excited in the **Frequency Sweep** simulation. In real life the direction of excitation would never be perfectly aligned with one plane and all modes would be excited to some extent.

We will simulate a frequency sweep with a shaker table using **Harmonic** study *Frequency sweep* with properties shown in Figure 12-10.

Frequency options   Harmonic Options

Figure 12-10: Frequency Options and Harmonic Options in Harmonic study simulating a Frequency Sweep.

Frequency Options define how many modes will be used in the Modal Superposition method. Harmonic Options define the range of frequencies in the simulated Frequency Sweep.

Frequency Options are identical to the settings of the already completed *Modal* study.

Damping in the **Harmonic** study must be defined as a modal damping as shown in Figure 12-11.

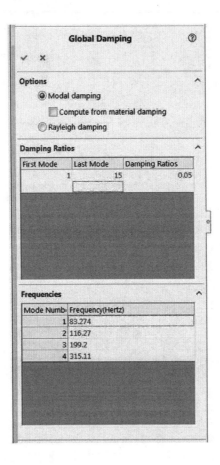

Figure 12-11: Modal damping definition for the three studies simulating a Frequency Sweep.

Modal damping is 5% for all studies. The Last Mode is listed here as 15 but only four modes are present in the analysis.

Defining the modal damping the same for all modes is conservative, meaning that displacement and stress results for higher modes may be overestimated. In reality damping in higher modes is usually higher because of more deformation present in those modes.

Use the same restraints and mesh as in the previously completed static and modal studies.

Figure 12-12 shows the **Base Excitation** definition in study *Frequency sweep* **Uniform Base Excitation** means that the same excitation is applied to all restraints which are active in the direction of excitation.

Read this message

Displacement

Direction normal to Top Plane

Amplitude 0.1mm

The amplitude does not change with frequency

Figure 12-12: Base excitation in study *Frequency sweep.*

The amplitude of displacement remains constant throughout the entire range of frequencies.

Notice an imprecise terminology of **Variation with Frequency**. The term **Linear** actually means constant amplitude throughout the range of frequencies.

Define **Results Options** as shown in Figure 12-13.

For specified solution steps

Relative

1000 steps

All Tracked Data Sensors

Figure 12-13: Results Options definition in *Frequency sweep* study.

Relative means that results are presented relative to the oscillating base.

The number of steps doesn't have to be 1000; it has to be equal to or higher than the number of steps that will be actually performed.

Construct **Response Graphs** of UY displacement amplitude recorded by the **Displacement Sensor** and P1 stress amplitude recorded by the **Stress Sensor**.

Definition of the **Response Graph** for P1 stress amplitude is shown in Figure 12-14.

Figure 12-14: Definition of the Response Graph shown here for P1 stress.

Select the vertex where the required sensor is located. P1stress is used because model's material is Gray Cast Iron.

Automatically created graphs may be saved as a csv file for processing in a spreadsheet (Figure 12-15).

Click File
Select
Save As csv

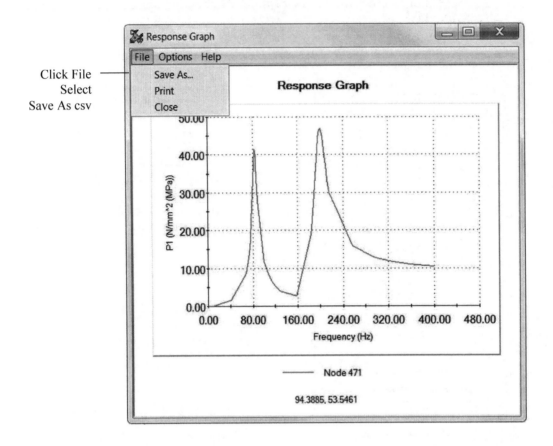

Figure 12-15: Saving the Response Graph for processing in another program.

Select csv format to export data to Excel. Selection of the csv data format is not shown in this illustration.

The graph in Figure 12-16 shows UY displacement magnitude as a function of frequency; it has been formatted in Excel.

Figure 12-16: Displacement amplitude as a function of excitation frequency. The excitation frequency changes within the range of the frequency sweep (0-400Hz).

The excitation frequency equal to the first modal frequency 84Hz produces an oscillation within the range of -0.73mm to +0.73mm.

The excitation is in the XY plane. Therefore, modes 2 and 4, which have shapes moving out of the XY plane are not excited even though their frequencies are within the range of the **Frequency Sweep**.

Review the Response Graph of the UZ displacement component and notice that UZ displacement is practically zero. The only reason some displacement is shown is due to discretization error which makes stiffness not exactly symmetric about the XY plane.

The graph in Figure 12-17 shows P1 stress as a function of frequency. It has also been formatted in Excel.

Frequency [Hz]

Figure 12-17: P1 stress amplitude in the indicated location as a function of excitation frequency. The excitation frequency changes within the range of the frequency sweep (0-400Hz).

The excitation frequency equal to the third modal frequency 199Hz produces P1 stress equal to 47MPa.

Excitation with frequencies equal to or very close to the modal frequency and along the corresponding direction of the modal shape is called **Resonance**. At resonance, inertial forces cancel with stiffness forces and the vibration response is controlled only by damping. This causes a very significant increase of displacement and stress amplitudes at resonant frequencies.

Compare graphs in Figure 12-16 and Figure 12-17 and notice that while the displacement response is higher for the first resonant frequency (Mode 1), the stress response is higher for the second resonant frequency (Mode 3).

Summary of studies completed

Model	Configuration	Study Name	Study Type
ELBOW PIPE.sldprt	*Default*	*Gravity*	Static
		Modal	Frequency
		Frequency sweep	Harmonic

Figure 12-18: Names and types of studies completed in this chapter.

13: Omega square harmonic force excitation

Topics covered

- ❑ Unbalanced rotating machinery
- ❑ Resonance
- ❑ Modal damping
- ❑ Omega square excitation
- ❑ Steady state response

Procedure

CENTRIFUGE assembly presents a schematic centrifuge model (Figure 13-1).

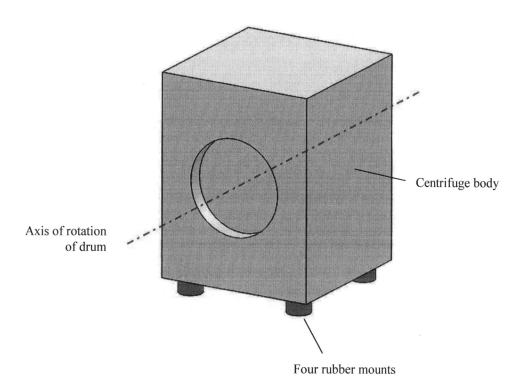

Figure 13-1: The centrifuge sits on four rubber mounts. The drum rotates about the horizontal axis. The motion of the centrifuge is restricted to the vertical direction.

The drum is merged with the body in this schematic model representation.

The drum has a dynamic imbalance of 5kg at a radius of 100mm. The centrifugal imbalance force F is a function of angular velocity, ω:

$$F = me\omega^2$$

$$m = 5kg \; - \; imbalanced \; mass$$

$$e = 0.1m \; - \; eccentricity$$

$$\omega \quad rad/s - angular \; velocity$$

The operating speed of the centrifuge is 2000RPM which corresponds to a frequency of 33.3Hz. Our objective is to find the amplitude of vibration of the centrifuge body as a function of the angular velocity when the machine slowly reaches its operating speed. This is **a Steady State Harmonic Response** problem requiring a **Harmonic** study.

Create a **Harmonic** study titled *Centrifuge* and define restraints as shown in Figure 13-2.

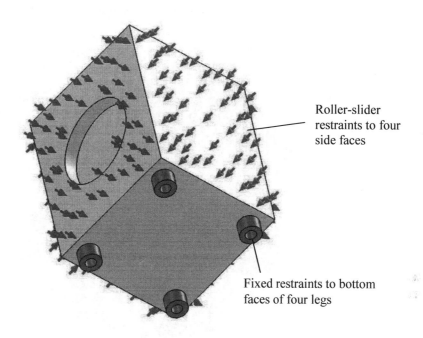

Roller-slider restraints to four side faces

Fixed restraints to bottom faces of four legs

Figure 13-2: Restraints applied to the assembly model allow for vertical movement of the body accompanied by deformation of the rubber mounts.

Roller-slider restraints applied to two perpendicular faces would suffice.

Symbols of Fixed restraints defined on the bottom faces of the four rubber mounts are not shown.

Even though geometry is very simple, meshing requires some planning. If the entire model is meshed with a default element size, rubber legs will be meshed with highly distorted elements; consequently leg stiffness will be modeled incorrectly: it will be too high. An incorrect mesh is shown in Figure 13-3.

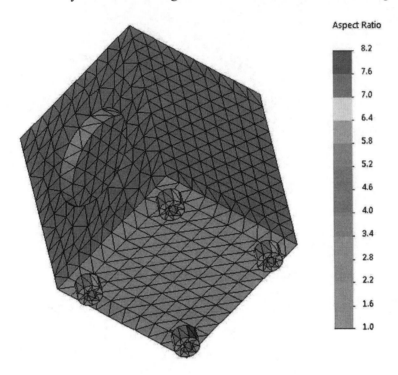

Figure 13-3: Incorrect mesh created using the default element size.

Aspect Ratio plot locates highly distorted elements on all four legs.

The correct mesh must have small elements meshing legs while the centrifuge body may be meshed with large elements. This may be accomplished by defining **Mesh Control** on legs which are components of the assembly. Additionally, **Incompatible Mesh** in **Component Contact** options may be specified to avoid unnecessarily small elements in the centrifuge body close to legs. Mesh design is shown in Figure 13-4.

Figure 13-4: Correct mesh created with small elements meshing rubber legs and large elements meshing the centrifuge body.

Examine the detail and notice that nodes in rubber legs do not match the nodes in the centrifuge body because Incompatible mesh has been specified in Component Contact.

Before running the study, we'll run a modal analysis to investigate frequencies in the range of 0-2000RPM. Run a modal analysis from inside the **Harmonic** study and review the frequencies of the first five modes. Specify five modes instead of the default fifteen modes in the **Frequency Options** of the **Harmonic** study.

Results of the modal analysis are shown in Figure 13-5.

Mode No.	Frequency(Rad/sec)	Frequency(Hertz)	Period(Seconds)
1	52.365	8.3342	0.11999
2	3250.3	517.3	0.0019331
3	3253	517.74	0.0019315
4	3253.6	517.83	0.0019311
5	3260	518.85	0.0019273

Modal shape 1 with frequency of 8.3Hz. Deformation is limited to the rubber legs. The centrifuge performs oscillations in the vertical direction.

Only mode 1 is in the range of the operating frequencies: 0 – 33Hz

Figure 13-5: Results of the modal analysis.

Animate modes 2-5 to see that they correspond to local deformation of the rubber legs.

Using the results of the modal analysis we know that there is only one mode in the range of operating frequencies 0 -33Hz. Therefore, we reduce the number of modes to just one in **Frequency Options** and specify this range in **Harmonic Options** (Figure 13-6).

Frequency options   Harmonic Options

Figure 13-6: Options of the Harmonic study.

The operating frequency limits correspond to the range 0-2000RPM.

Define Modal Damping as 5%, which corresponds to high damping in the rubber material. The damping definition is shown in Figure 13-5.

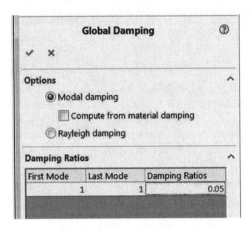

Figure 13-7: Definition of Modal Damping.

Damping only needs to be defined for one mode.

The load F has to be defined as a square function of angular velocity; $= me\omega^2$. Using a schematic representation of the centrifuge as in the assembly model CENTRIFUGE, we may represent the imbalanced force in a simplified manner by defining a load to the top face. Open the spreadsheet CENTRIFUGE, copy the highlighted table and follow the steps shown in Figure 13-6 to define the load.

(1a)
Select the top
face of the
centrifuge

(2)
Enter normal
force of 1N

(3)
Select
Curve, Edit

(1b)
Top face of the
centrifuge
loaded with 1N
normal force

Type in or paste this table from
CENTRIFUGE.xlsx

Figure 13-8: Definition of the imbalanced load.

1N is a multiplier to the Y column of the table copied from the
CENTRIFUGE.xlsx spreadsheet. The Frequency curve window had been
modified to show all rows in the table.

Go to the CAD model to review the **Sensor** defined in one of the top corners of the centrifuge body. Define the **Results Options** shown in Figure 13-9.

Figure 13-9: Definition of Results Options.

This is done in preparation to graphing the magnitude of displacement as a function of the angular velocity. Even though the end step is defined here as 1000, the analysis will complete in only 37 steps.

Review Sensor defined in SOLIDWORKS assembly model; it is located in one of the top corners but could have been placed anywhere on the centrifuge body.

Solve the **Harmonic** study and define a response graph showing the amplitude of displacements as a function of the angular velocity (Figure 13-10).

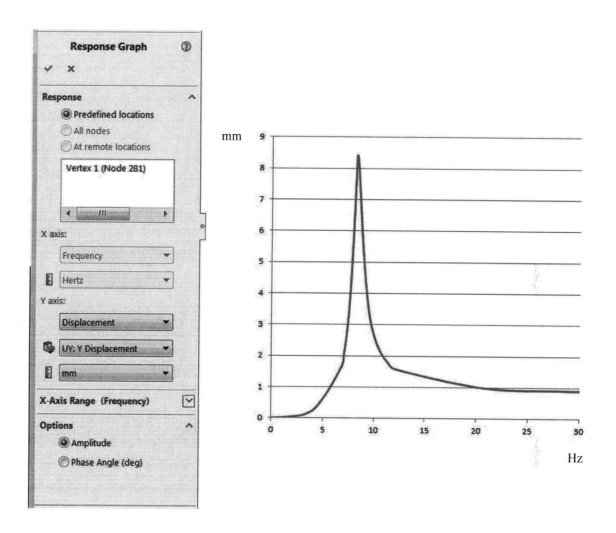

Figure 13-10: Amplitude of vertical displacement as a function of the excitation frequency.

The graph has been formatted in Excel.

The one peak in Figure 13-8 corresponds to the only natural frequency, 9.2Hz, present in the analyzed range of excitations. The maximum displacement amplitude is ~8mm and it happens when the excitation frequency equals the natural frequency 9.2Hz or 552RPM.

Notice that the amplitude reaches a constant value for excitation frequencies much higher than the resonant frequency, just like in the case of base excitation with constant displacement amplitude.

The displacement amplitude for omega square excitation for the excitation frequency much higher than the excitation frequency has analytical solution:

$$d = \frac{me}{M} = 0.77mm$$

$$m = 5kg \; - \; imbalanced \; mass$$

$$e = 0.1m \; - \; eccentricity$$

$$M = 645kg - mass \; of \; centrifuge \; body$$

You'll have to extend the range of the excitation frequency to 4000RPM to see the displacement amplitude converging to 0.77mm.

Summary of studies completed

Model	Configuration	Study Name	Study Type
CENTRIFUGE.sldasm	*Default*	*Centrifuge*	Harmonic

Figure 13-11: Names and types of studies completed in this chapter.

14: Time response analysis, resonance, beating

Topics covered

- ❑ Time Response analysis
- ❑ Base excitation
- ❑ Resonance
- ❑ Modal damping
- ❑ Beating phenomenon
- ❑ Transient response
- ❑ Steady state response
- ❑ Mass participation

A support bracket is formed from a steel sheet in the SUPPORT model, which lends itself well to a surface model shown in Figure 14-1. The wide end is fixed over the area defined by the split face.

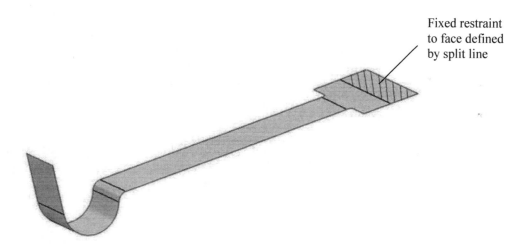

Fixed restraint to face defined by split line

Figure 14-1: The SUPPORT model consists entirely of surfaces.

Restraint symbols are not shown. The face shown with hatching lines is where Fixed restraint is defined.

The SUPPORT bracket is subjected to harmonic base excitation with displacement amplitude of 0.05mm (Figure 14-2).

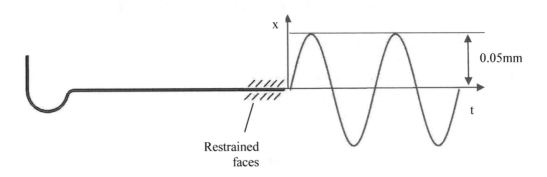

Figure 14-2: Harmonic base excitation applied to the SUPPORT model.

The restrained face performs harmonic oscillations with displacement amplitude of 0.05mm.

We want to investigate the bracket response to the harmonic base excitation shown in Figure 14-2 when the frequency of excitation is close to the natural frequency of the SUPPORT model. This exercise will serve to study the differences between **Modal Time History (Time Response)** and **Harmonic (Frequency Response)** analyses. Both these analyses are based on the **Modal Superposition Method** and require the pre-requisite results of a **Frequency (Modal)** analysis.

Create a **Frequency** study titled *Modal* and define **Fixed** restraint as shown in Figure 14-1. Define the shell element thickness as 3mm and mesh the model with the default element size.

Run the *Modal* study to find the first four modes shown in Figure 14-3.

Mode 1: 15.87Hz   Mode 2: 105.0Hz

Mode 3: 133.6Hz   Mode 2: 228.3Hz

Figure 14-3: The first four modes of the SUPPORT model.

Review the above mode shapes. The undeformed shape is not shown here to avoid overcrowding of this illustration.

A review of the modal shapes demonstrates that the first modal shape is coincident with the direction of the base excitation shown in Figure 14-2. Therefore, a base excitation with a frequency close to 15.87Hz will excite this mode.

Create a **Modal Time History** study titled *01 time response 0%*; there will be no damping present in this study. Define study properties as shown in Figure 14-4.

Frequency Options   Dynamic Options

Figure 14-4: Properties of Modal Time History study *01 time response 0%.*

Only one mode is specified in the Frequency Options.

We'll study the model's response to base excitation with frequencies close to the first natural frequency. The first mode will dominate the vibration response; therefore, only this first mode is specified in **Frequency Options**. In the **Dynamic Options** specify the duration of the analysis as 2s with a time step of 0.002s which consequently defines 1000 solution steps (Figure 14-4).

The assumption that the vibration response may be represented by the response of the first mode will only work well to study the response when the excitation frequency is close to the natural frequency. It wouldn't be valid for a more general study.

In the **Modal Time History** study, the base excitation must be specified as an explicit function of time. Since the base excitation is a harmonic function of time we may use a pre-defined **Harmonic Loading** to define the **Time Curve**. Details of the base excitation definition are explained in Figure 14-5.

Figure 14-5: Base excitation definition.

Amplitude is defined as 1 in the Time Curve window. This is multiplied by the displacement defined in the Uniform Base Excitation window.

The End time is slightly longer than the analysis duration specified in the study properties.

The excitation is applied to all locations restrained in the direction normal to the **Top** reference plane. Therefore, even though the **Uniform Base Excitation** symbol is located in the geometric center of the model, the excitation is applied only to the restrained face.

Review the **Sensor** definition as shown in Figure 14-6.

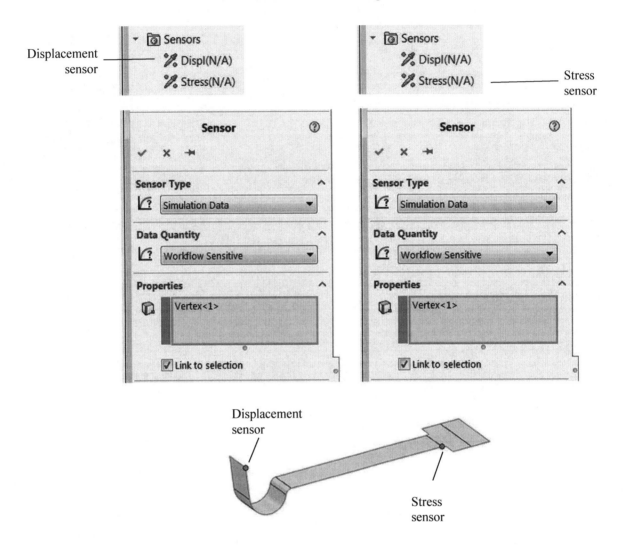

Figure 14-6: Two sensors defined in the model: displacement sensor and stress sensor.

This is for review only; the SUPPORT model comes with this sensor already defined. Even though both windows show Vertex<1> as the selected entities, these selections refer to different entities as shown by the call-outs.

Figure 14-6 shows two sensors; the sensor on the left called "Displ" will be used to construct displacement response graphs. The sensor on the right called "Stress" is located close to where the maximum stress will be found and will be used to construct stress response graphs.

Define **Result Options** as shown in Figure 14-7.

For specified
solution steps

All Tracked
Data Sensors

Figure 14-7: Result Options definition; make the above selections, accept default solution steps.

"All Tracked Data Sensors" selection means both sensors.

Run the solution and define the response graphs as shown in figure 14-8.

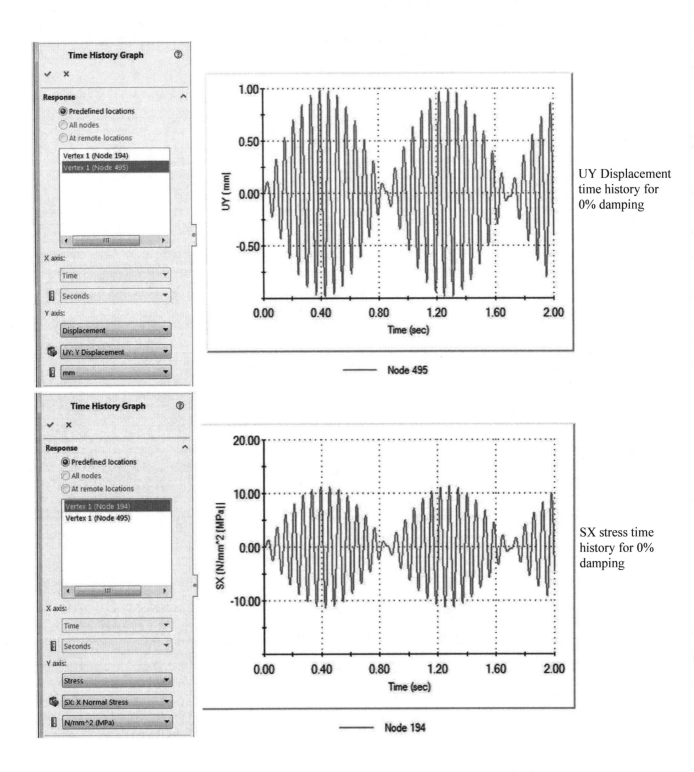

UY Displacement time history for 0% damping

SX stress time history for 0% damping

Figure 14-8: Time History of UY displacement and SX stress in the locations of the sensors with 0% damping in the model.

The total time of 2s corresponds to the time duration defined in the study Properties.

The SX stress sensor registers stress on the top of the shell element.

The graphs in Figure 14-8 illustrate the phenomenon called **Beating**. These changes happen for as long as the base excitation is active. The vibration response never reaches a steady state where the amplitude of vibration would stabilize. Remember that no damping has been defined in this study.

To study the effect of damping, copy study *01 time response 0%* into study *02 time response 4%*. The difference between these two studies will be the damping. In study *02 time response 4%* define **Modal Damping** as 4% (Figure 14-9).

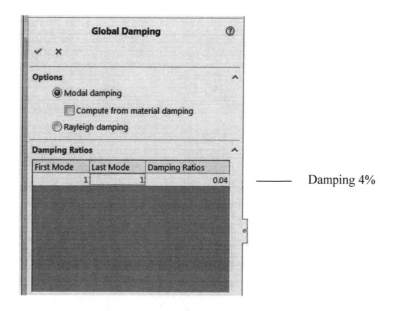

Figure 14-9: Modal Damping definition.

Study is based on one mode; therefore, damping is also defined only for one mode.

Obtain the solution of study *02 time response 4%* and review the displacement and time histories the same way as was shown in Figure 14-10.

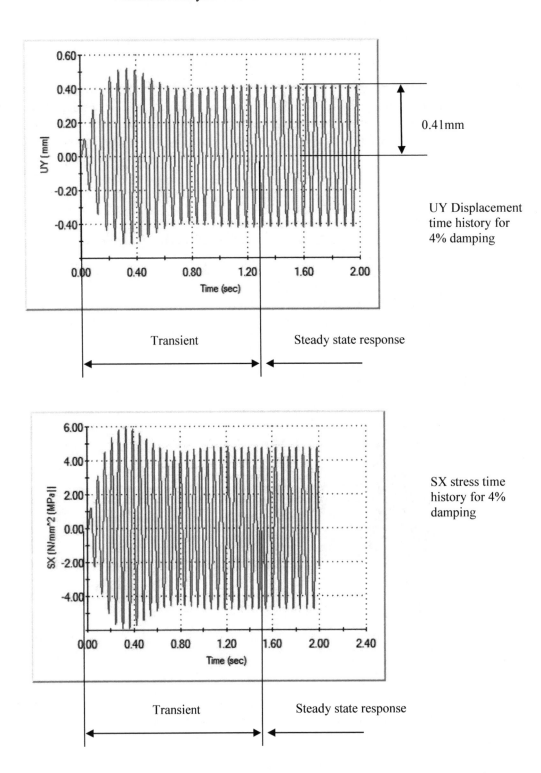

Figure 14-10: Time History of UY displacement and SX stress in the locations of sensors with 4% damping; graph definition windows are the same as shown in Figure 14-8.

The transient response disappears after ~1.5s and the displacement amplitude reaches a steady state of 0.41mm.

Here is a summary of both cases: without damping, and with 4% modal damping.

Undamped response

The maximum UY displacement amplitude without damping is ~1mm. This maximum displacement repeats periodically for as long as the base excitation continues. The maximum displacement amplitude amplification is 1/0.05=20. It is so large because the excitation frequency is very close to the natural frequency; the system is very close to resonance. The time distance between the maximum amplitudes is called the **Beating Period**. The **Beating Period** T depends on the natural frequency of the system f_n, and on the frequency of excitation f, which in our case gives the **Beating Period** equal to 0.88s:

$$T = \frac{1}{|fn - f|} = \frac{1}{|15.87 - 17|} = 0.88s$$

Damped response

The maximum UY displacement amplitude with 4% modal damping happens at t=0.3s when the amplitude reaches ~0.52mm. The maximum displacement amplitude amplification is ~10 and periodic amplifications of displacement amplitude diminish with time. The **Beating Period** remains the same as in the case of undamped vibration but it continues for about 1.5 seconds. Then the amplitude of vibration reaches **Steady State** when the amplitude stabilizes at 0.41mm.

We'll now perform a **Frequency Response** study on the same model. To produce results that relate closely to the **Time Response** studies, we will again use only one mode, and a range of excitation frequencies of 0-25Hz to only cover the first natural frequency of 15.87Hz. Create a **Harmonic** study titled *03 frequency response 4%* and define the study properties as shown in Figure 14-11.

Frequency Options   Advanced Options

Figure 14-11: Harmonic study options.

Click Advanced Options in Harmonic Options to open the Advanced tab. Harmonic Options and Advanced Options windows have been modified in a graphics program to better fit this page.

In the **Frequency Options**, specify only one mode. This way the study will only be based on the first mode (15.87Hz). In the **Harmonic Options**, specify the range of excitation frequencies as 0-25Hz. This captures both the natural frequency (15.84Hz) and the excitation frequency (17Hz) used in the previous **Modal Time History** studies. In the **Advanced Options**, specify the number of points to be 50, a bandwidth of 1, and linear interpolation. This way the frequency range will be covered in 101 equal sized frequency steps with no bias around the natural frequency.

The number of frequency steps performed is 101: 50 steps below the natural frequency, and 50 steps above the natural frequency. The step count includes the step at time t = 0s; therefore, the total number of steps is 101.

Define **Base Excitation** and **Result Options** the same as in the **Time Response** studies. Define a **Modal Damping** of 4%. Run the study and construct the **Response Graph** showing the UY displacement amplitude as a function of the excitation frequency (Figure 14-12).

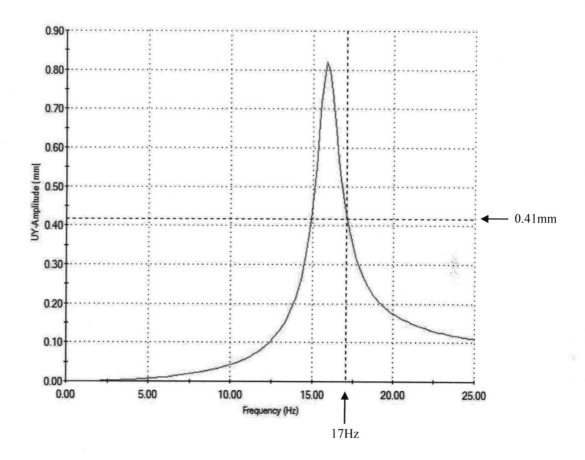

Figure 14-12: Displacement amplitude as a function of the excitation frequency.

The dotted lines cross at the point that corresponds to the steady state response in Figure 14-10.

Figure 14-12 shows the steady state displacement amplitude for all frequencies within the range of 0-25Hz, including the frequency of 17Hz, which was the excitation frequency in the **Time Response** studies. Review the graph and notice that the steady state displacement amplitude for the excitation frequency is at 17Hz is 0.41mm. This is the same amplitude as the steady state amplitude found in the *02 time response 4%* study.

The graph in Figure 14-12 could be constructed using steady state results of a large number (here one hundred and one) of time response analyses, clearly a very time consuming approach. The **Frequency Response** analyses provided these results within one study.

Now, copy the study *02 time response 4%* into *04 time response 4% resonance*. In this new study change the frequency of harmonic excitation from 17Hz to 15.87Hz to make it equal to the first natural frequency of the model within two decimals of accuracy. The displacement time history in the location of the sensor is shown in Figure 14-13.

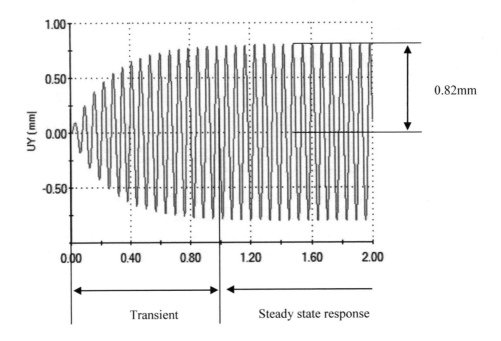

Figure 14-13: Displacement time history for harmonic excitation with a frequency of 15.87Hz which is equal to the natural frequency.

After ~ the system reaches steady state, where the amplitude stabilizes at 0.82mm.

The steady state amplitude of vibration in resonance is 0.82mm. The **Frequency Response** study *03 frequency response 4%* gives the same results. Go back to the graph in Figure 14-12 and notice that the displacement amplitude at resonance is ~0.82mm.

Summary of studies completed

Model	Configuration	Study Name	Study Type
SUPPORT.sldprt	*Default*	*Modal*	Frequency
		01 time response 0%	Modal Time History
		02 time response 4%	Modal Time History
		03 frequency response 4%	Harmonic
		04 time response 4% resonance	Modal Time History

Figure 14- 14: Names and types of studies completed in this chapter.

15: Vibration absorption

Topics covered

- Torsional vibration
- Resonance
- Modal damping
- Vibration absorption
- Frequency Response

Procedure

Open assembly model VIB ABSORBER and examine the three assembly configurations shown in Figure 15-1.

Configuration
01 one disk

Configuration
02 absorber

Configuration
03 full model

Figure 15-1: Three configurations of the VIB ABSORBER assembly.

Little tabs on both disks help place sensors and aid in visualizing the torsional modes of vibration.

The assembly comes with sensors defined as shown in Figure 15-2.

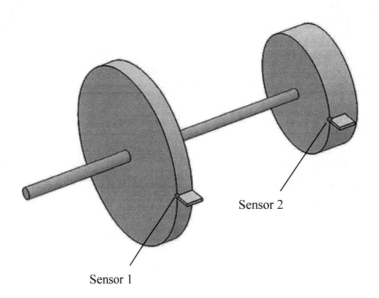

Figure 15-2: Sensor locations in the VIB ABSORBER model.

Sensors are located at the base of each tab.

We start an analysis in the *01 one disk* configuration to model the torsional vibration of one disk subjected to a harmonic torque load. The torque amplitude is 10Nm and does not change with the frequency of oscillations which is 0-80Hz. While 0-80Hz is the range of excitation frequencies, we are particularly interested in the steady state displacement amplitude at a frequency equal to 28Hz. For this purpose we use a **Harmonic** study.

Create a **Harmonic** study titled *01 one disk*. The disk is restrained as shown in Figure 15-3. The cylindrical faces of the shaft and disk are restrained in the radial direction using an **On Cylindrical Faces** restraint. The end face of the shaft has a **Fixed** restraint applied.

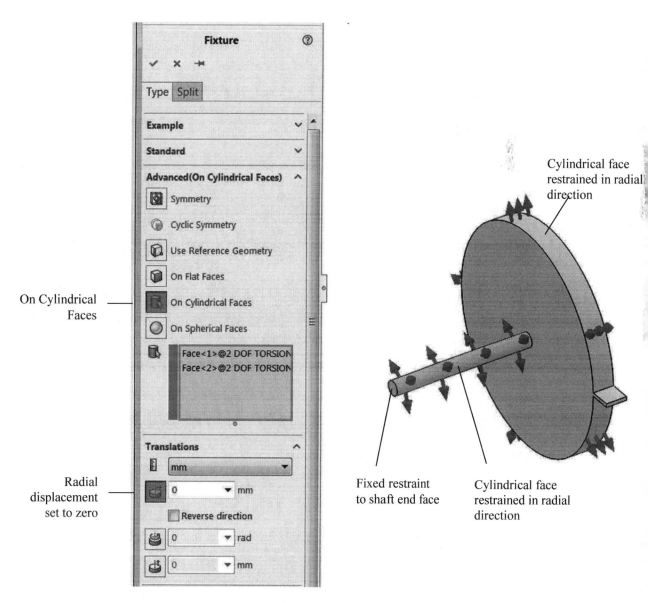

Figure 15-3: Both cylindrical surfaces are restrained in the radial direction.

The Fixed restraint definition window and symbol are not shown.

As a result of the restraints shown in Figure 15-3, the disk has only one mode of vibration in the range 0-80Hz. This is a torsional mode with a frequency of 28.1Hz. You may want to confirm this by running a modal analysis.

The disk is subjected to an oscillating torque of 10Nm as shown in Figure 15-4.

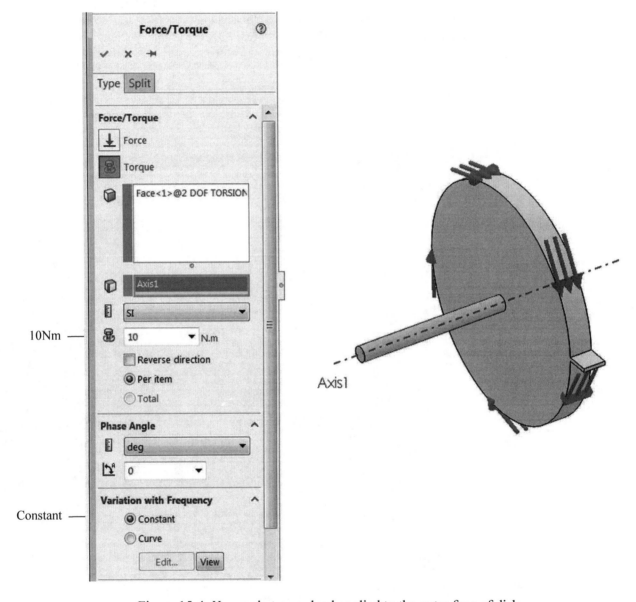

Figure 15-4: Harmonic torque load applied to the outer face of disk.

Selecting Constant for Variation with Frequency means that the torque amplitude does not change with the excitation frequency.

Define study properties as shown in Figure 15-5.

One mode —

Harmonic Options

Frequency Options   Advanced Options

Figure 15-5: Properties of Harmonic study *01 one disk.*

Notice the modified Advanced Options: 50 points for each frequency, bandwidth 1, Linear interpolation selected.

In this exercise we are interested in the vibration response between natural frequencies. This is why **Advanced Options** have to be modified as follows.

Considering that only one mode is specified, 50 points defined in **Advanced Options** means that 50 frequency steps will be performed before reaching the natural frequency, another 50 after that and one for the natural frequency. Linear interpolations means that frequency steps won't be biased towards natural frequencies but will be evenly distributed over the frequency range 0-80Hz.

Define modal damping as 1% (Figure 15-6).

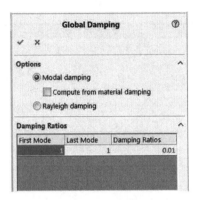

Figure 15-6: Modal damping defined as 1%.

Only one mode is shown in the Global Damping window because only one mode has been specified in the Frequency Options.

Define the **Result Options** as shown in Figure 15-7.

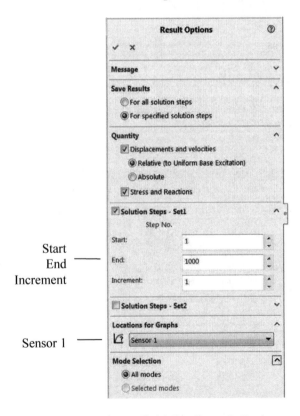

Start
End
Increment

Sensor 1

Figure 15-7: Definition of Result Options.

Only one sensor is available in the 01 one disk study; it is associated with the 01 one disk assembly configuration.

A start step of 1 and an end step of 1000 with increments of 1 means that the graphs may contain no more than 1000 points. It is not the number of actual time steps.

Mesh the model with the default element size and obtain the solution. Define a **Response Graph** as shown in Figure 15-8:

Vertex 1 is in
Sensor 1 location

UY
displacement
component

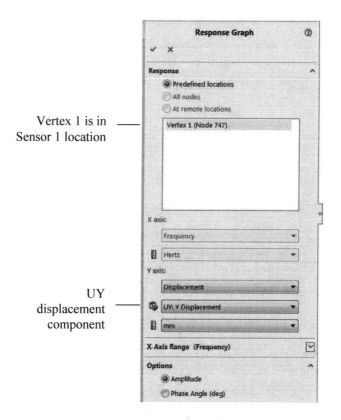

Figure 15-8: Definition of the displacement amplitude response graph.

We use a linear displacement on the circumference of the disk as a measure of angular rotation.

The UY displacement component selected in the **Response Graph** in Figure 15-8 is a linear displacement in the circumferential direction. If desired, it can be translated into angular displacement as shown in Figure 15-9.

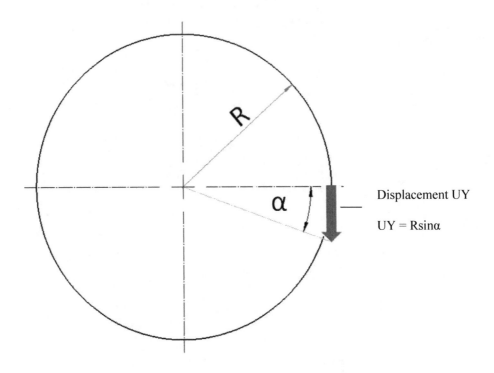

Displacement UY

$UY = R\sin\alpha$

Figure 15-9: UY displacement can be translated into an angular displacement.

The equation is valid only for small displacements.

The UY displacement amplitude frequency response graph is shown in Figure 15-10.

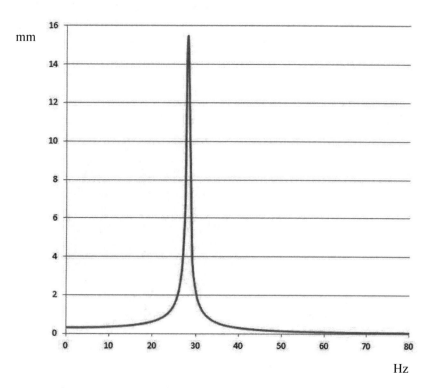

Figure 15-10: UY displacement amplitude frequency response. The peak corresponds to the natural frequency of 28.1Hz.

This graph has been formatted in Excel.

Damping in the system is low (1%); therefore, the maximum displacement amplitude happens when the excitation frequency equals the natural frequency. In other words, the system experiences resonance at 28.1Hz.

Now, let's imagine a situation where the disk is subjected to harmonic oscillations with a frequency of 28.1Hz which is the resonant frequency. We find the displacement amplitude too large and want to reduce it. We'll do that by attaching a **vibration absorber**, the natural frequency of which will be equal to the frequency of excitation. Notice that this is the frequency of the absorber before it is attached to the disk.

See the absorber before attaching it to the disk. Change to configuration *02 absorber*. Create a **Frequency** study *02 absorber*; apply restraints to the shaft and to the disk the same way as shown in Figure 15-3 and find the first mode of vibration to confirm that it is a torsional mode with a frequency of 28.1Hz (Figure 15-11).

Model name: 2DOF TORSION
Study name: 02 absorber(-02 absorber-)
Plot type: Frequency Displacement1
Mode Shape : 1 Value =   28.101 Hz
Deformation scale: 0.0696071

Undeformed shape

Deformed shape

Figure 15-11: The first mode of vibration of the absorber: a torsional mode with a frequency of 28.1Hz.

The circular shape makes visualization of the torsional mode difficult. Tabs help the visualization.

The apparent growth of the disk diameter visible during modal animation is caused by the fact that displacement trajectories are straight lines tangent to the circumference of disk. This is an inherent property of linear analysis.

Now we are ready for the main part of this exercise where we analyze the effect of the vibration absorber attached to the disk. Switch to assembly configuration *03 full model* and create a **Harmonic** study titled *03 full model*. In this configuration, the assembly consists of the disk and the absorber.

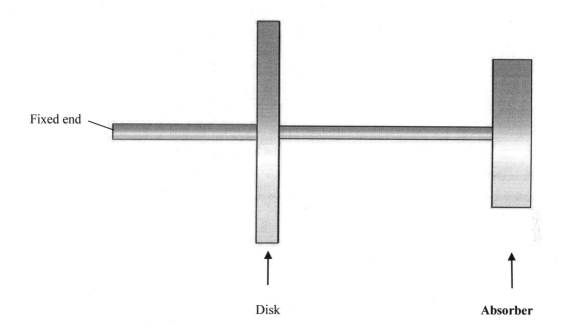

Figure 15-12: The assembly model with the vibration absorber attached to the disk.

Disk is subjected to oscillating torque as shown in Figure 15-4.

All cylindrical faces of disks and shafts are restrained in the radial direction.

Define a **Harmonic** study with properties shown in Figure 15-13; two modes are now specified.

Two modes

Frequency Options   Harmonic Options

Figure 15-13: Properties of the Harmonic study for the model in the 03 full model configuration.

Advanced Options are not shown; make them the same as in Figure 15-5.

Apply restraints as shown in Figure 15-12. Define a harmonic torque excitation the same as in Figure 15-4 and **Results Options** as shown in Figure 15-14.

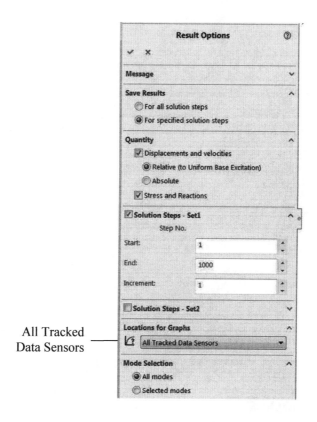

Figure 15-14: Results Option for the *03 full model* configuration.

"All Tracked Data Sensors" means Sensor1 and Sensor2.

The system has two natural frequencies in the range of 0-80Hz. Modal frequencies and shapes are shown in Figure 15-15.

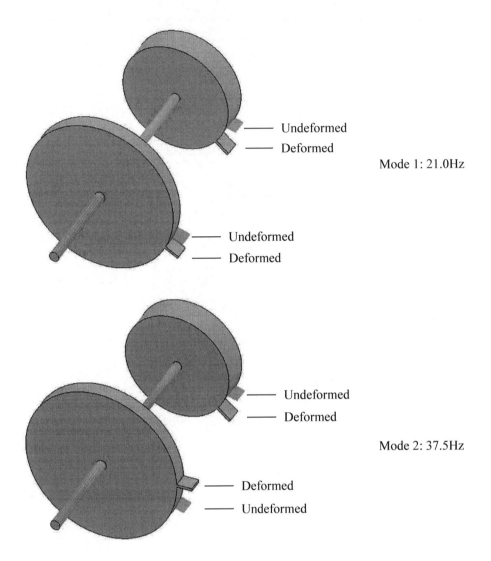

Figure 15-15: Two modes of vibration in the 0-80Hz range are torsional modes.

Animate the modal shapes to see that in mode 1 both disks oscillate in the same direction and in mode 2 they oscillate in the opposite directions.

Run the solution and notice that it proceeds in 151 steps because the **Advanced Options** in the study properties specify 50 points for each frequency (Figure 15-16).

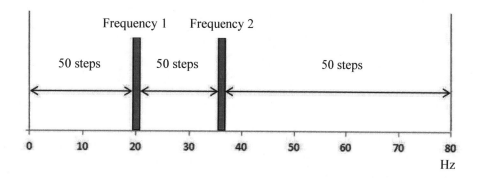

Figure 15-16: The range of frequencies is divided in three parts: 50 steps each.

The step count includes the step at time t=0; therefore, the total count is 151.

Once the solution completes, construct the **Response Graph** showing UY displacement amplitude as a function of the excitation frequency.

Response graphs formatted in Excel are shown in Figure 15-17.

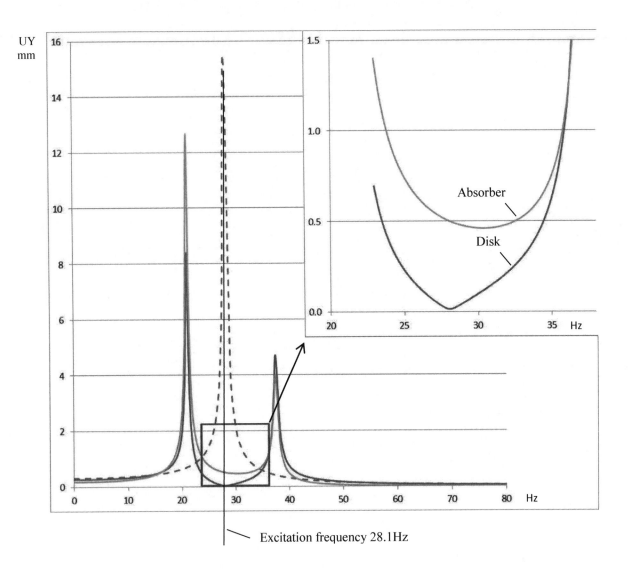

Figure 15-17: A summary of UY amplitude frequency response from the single disk study (dotted line) in *study 01 one disk*, and the disk with the absorber in study *03 full model*.

The main graph summarizes results from studies *01 one disk* (dotted line) and *03 full model* (solid lines). The dotted line repeats the results shown in Figure 15-10. The insert shows results from study *03 full model* in the narrow range of frequencies 24-36Hz.

It can be seen that attaching the absorber de-tunes the system from the resonant frequency of 28.1Hz. The system now has two resonant frequencies in the range 0-80Hz: 21.0Hz and 37.5Hz as shown by the two peaks in Figure 15-17 and modal shapes in Figure 15-14.

The results of the **Harmonic** study *03 full model* provide an overview of the system response in the specified range of frequencies. We are particularly interested in the frequency of 28.1Hz which is the frequency of the torque excitation and the frequency of the absorber before attaching it to the main disk. As Figure 15-17 illustrates, when the absorber is attached to the main disk and the main disk is excited with a 28.1Hz frequency, the vibration of the main disk stops at this frequency of excitation; see the insert in Figure 15-17 showing very low amplitude of vibration. We say that the vibration has been "absorbed" by the added vibrating system, hence the name **Vibration Absorber**.

Controlling vibrations by means of adding an absorber is practical only in cases where the frequency of excitation is constant and adding components is possible. Assembly model 2DOF TORSION presents an idealized system performing angular vibration. We may treat it as a discrete vibrating system because:

1. The mass moment of inertia of shafts is low as compared to the mass moment of inertia of disks (the main disk and absorber). The torsional stiffness of disks is high as compared to the torsional stiffness of shafts. Therefore, we may assume that shafts are responsible for stiffness properties and disks are responsible for inertial properties of this system.

2. The system is subjected to restraints in such a way as to have two separate torsional modes of vibration within the range of the investigated frequencies.

The analysis conducted on VIB ABSORBER assembly model illustrates the principle of vibration absorbing which applies to systems performing linear and angular vibration.

The analysis does not address important problems such as stress and fatigue. You may want to analyze stresses as function of frequency to see that yield strength of material is exceeded at resonance.

Summary of studies completed

Model	Configuration	Study Name	Study Type
VIB ABSORBER.sldasm	*01 one disk*	*01 one disk*	Harmonic
	02 absorber	*02 absorber*	Frequency
	03 full model	*03 full model*	Harmonic

Figure 15-18: Names and types of studies completed in this chapter.

16: Random vibration

Topics covered

- ❑ Random vibration
- ❑ Power Spectral Density
- ❑ RMS results
- ❑ PSD results
- ❑ Modal excitation

Random vibration

Random vibrations are non-periodic. Knowing the history of random vibration, we can predict the probability of occurrence of acceleration, velocity and displacement magnitudes, but cannot predict the precise magnitude at a specific instance in time.

Random vibration is composed of a continuous spectrum of frequencies. The huge amount of time history data makes it impractical or impossible to solve random vibration problems using time response analysis.

For most structural vibrations, the excitation, such as a base acceleration, alternates about zero. Consequently, mean values characterizing the excitation, as well as responses to that excitation such as displacement or stress, are equal to zero and can't be used to characterize random vibration responses. For this reason, results of a random vibration analysis are given in the form of Root Mean Square (RMS) values.

To explain the concept of an RMS value, refer to the graph in Figure 16-1 which shows the acceleration time history (acceleration as a function of time) of random vibration expressed in units of gravitational acceleration [G].

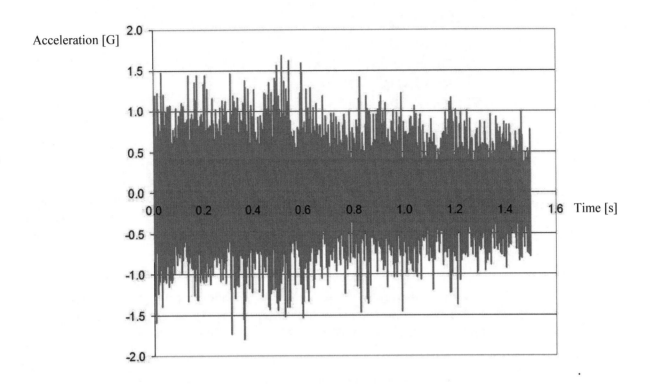

Figure 16-1: An example of acceleration time history data collected during 1.5s.

Considering the sampling rate of 5000 samples per second, this time history curve contains 7500 data samples. This acceleration time history has a zero mean.

The acceleration time history shown in Figure 16-1 has a zero mean value. However, if we multiply the function by itself, we obtain a function with a positive value. This squared function will be well suited to characterize the acceleration time history because its mean value will not be zero. This mean value of square acceleration time history is the mean square value and has units of $[G^2]$.

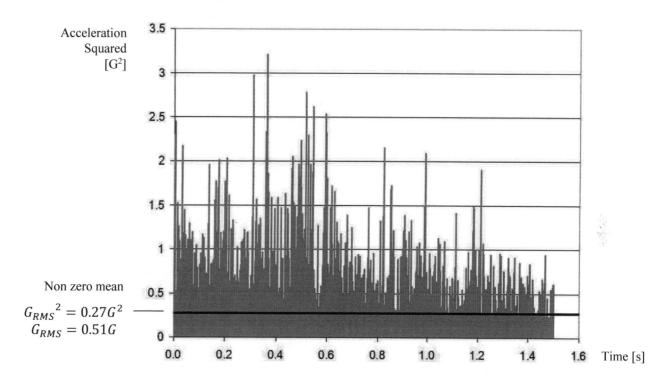

Acceleration Squared $[G^2]$

Non zero mean

$$G_{RMS}^2 = 0.27G^2$$
$$G_{RMS} = 0.51G$$

Time [s]

Figure 16-2: Squaring the acceleration time history function shown in Figure 16-1 produces a function with a non-zero mean.

Non-zero mean can be used to characterize the acceleration time history.

As shown in Figure 16-2, calculating the mean square value gives $G_{RMS}^2 = 0.27G$. The square root of the mean square value gives $G_{RMS} = 0.51G$.

The square root of the mean value is the root-mean-square (RMS) acceleration and has units of [G]. The same applies to RMS displacement, velocity, stress etc.

In random vibration, the magnitudes of acceleration, velocity, displacement etc. all follow a normal distribution. The RMS value corresponds to one standard deviation σ characterizing the normal distribution. To explain this, we refer again to Figure 16-2. The acceleration, as characterized by the given acceleration time history, has a 68% probability of remaining between -0.51G and +0.51G. Consequently, it has a 32% probability of being less than -0.51G or more than 0.51G.

Acceleration Power Spectral Density

Let's assume that the acceleration time history in Figure 16-1 is a stationary random process where probability numbers characterizing this process do not change with time. In this case, the acceleration time history can be used to calculate the **Acceleration Power Spectral Density (PSD)** curve: the variation of any property with respect to frequency is called "spectrum."

The overall G_{RMS}^2 of random vibrations shown in Figure 16-2 is $0.27G^2$. However, random vibration is composed of a large number of frequencies. Let us say we wish to investigate G_{RMS}^2 individually for a number of frequencies in the range from 0 to 2000Hz. Therefore, we divide the 0-2000Hz range into 20 sections (bins), each 100Hz wide, and calculate G_{RMS}^2 characterizing each section by filtering out all frequencies falling outside of the section (Figure 16-3).

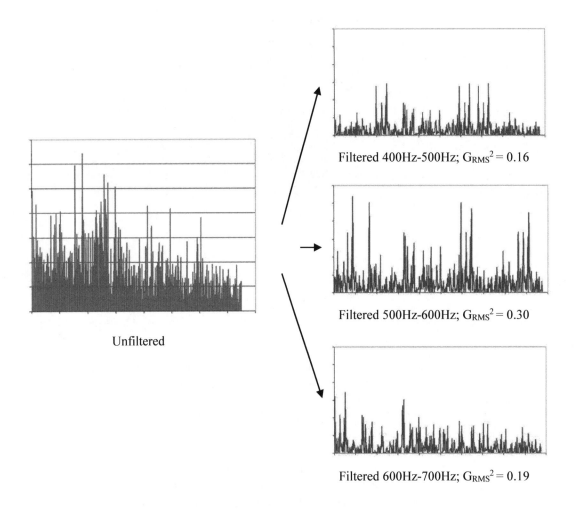

Filtered 400Hz-500Hz; $G_{RMS}^2 = 0.16$

Filtered 500Hz-600Hz; $G_{RMS}^2 = 0.30$

Unfiltered

Filtered 600Hz-700Hz; $G_{RMS}^2 = 0.19$

Figure 16-3: G_{RMS}^2 calculated individually for specified frequency ranges.

The graph on the left shows the squared acceleration time history from Figure 16-2. Only three frequency ranges (sections) are illustrated here for brevity.

Having found G_{RMS}^2 values obtained for each frequency range, we can now calculate individual "densities" of G_{RMS}^2 in each section by dividing G_{RMS}^2 in each section by the width of the section. Results obtained for all sections may be plotted as a function of the frequency in the center of each section. This function is called the **Acceleration Power Spectral Density** (Figure 16-4).

Band pass filter	Band center	G_{RMS}^2	Bandwidth	Acceleration PSD
	Hz	$(G)^2$	Hz	$(G)^2/Hz$
400Hz - 500Hz	450	0.16	100	0.0016
500Hz - 600Hz	550	0.30	100	0.0030
600Hz - 700Hz	650	0.19	100	0.0019

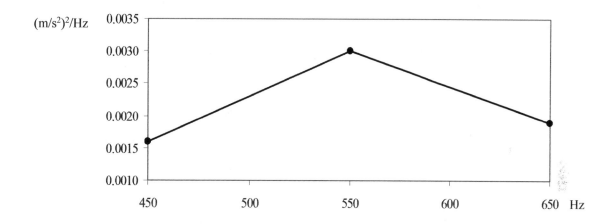

Figure 16-4: Constructing the Acceleration Power Spectral Density function (PSD).

Three points of the Acceleration PSD curve have been calculated by dividing G_{RMS}^2 in each section (each frequency range) by the width of the section.

The Acceleration Power Spectral Density (PSD) allows for a compression of data and is commonly used to characterize a random process. In particular, mechanical vibrations are commonly described by the Acceleration Power Spectral Density, which is easily generated by testing equipment. Design specifications and test results of devices subjected to random vibration are typically given in the form Acceleration PSD.

Analysis of random vibration of a hard drive head

Having completed this short introduction of random vibration, we now begin a random vibration analysis of a hard drive head. Open the assembly HD HEAD and examine two configurations: *01aligned* and *02 misaligned*.

The assembly contains only one part: HD HEAD; why can't we analyze the part instead of the assembly? In a **Random** study, the base excitation may only be applied along only one of the global X, Y or Z directions, which are aligned with the global coordinate system; no other directions are allowed. To apply a base excitation in any other direction, we must place the analyzed part in the desired position respective to the global coordinate system. The assembly enables positioning of the part with respect to the global coordinate system. In configuration *01 aligned* the HD HEAD is aligned with the global coordinate system. In configurations *02 misaligned*, it is rotated 45° about the X axis.

Configuration *01 aligned*

Configuration *02 misaligned*

Figure 16-5: Two assembly configurations are different only in the part position.

In configuration 01 aligned, all part reference planes are aligned with the corresponding assembly reference planes. In configuration 02 misaligned, the part is rotated 45° about the global X axis.

We'll start in configuration *01 aligned*. Create a **Frequency** study with properties shown in Figure 16-6; call the study *Modal*.

Upper bound frequency: 2500Hz

Figure 16-6: Properties of the Modal study.

All frequencies in the range of 0-2500Hz will be calculated.

Apply restraints as shown in Figure 16-7.

Figure 16-7: Restraints applied to the hard drive head model.

Define **Mesh Control** as shown in Figure 16-8 and mesh the model with the default element size.

Controlled faces —

Element size on the controlled — faces: 0.2mm

Figure 16-8: Mesh controls are applied to four round fillets.

Mesh controls specifies elements the size of 1/6 of the elements used to mesh the rest of the model.

Having defined mesh controls, use the default global element to mesh the model. If displacement results were our only objective, the default mesh would be acceptable for both **Frequency** and **Random** studies. However, since in the next study we intend to analyze displacements and stresses, mesh controls are required to ensure correct element shape and size in the area of stress concentrations. Prior to this exercise, analyses were run to find where mesh controls should be specified.

Solve the *Modal* study and review the results shown in Figure 16-9. Notice that there are four modes of vibration within the specified range of frequencies.

Mode 1: 405Hz

Mode 2: 1231Hz

Mode 3: 1321Hz

Mode 4: 2089Hz

<u>Figure 16-9: Modes of vibration within the range of 0 – 2500Hz.</u>

Vibration in mode 1 and 3 take place in the XY plane, vibrations in mode 2 and 4 take place in the XZ plane. The undeformed model is overlaid on the modal shape plots.

Proceeding to the analysis of the **Random** study, we could create a new **Dynamic** study independent from the completed **Frequency** study, this time with the **Random** option selected. However, a **Frequency** analysis would then have to be repeated within a **Dynamic Random** study. To avoid this repetition, we can copy the results of the **Frequency** study into a **Dynamic Random** study as shown in Figure 16-10.

Figure 16-10: Results of a Frequency study can be copied to a new Dynamic study.

Right-click the Modal study folder and select Copy to New Dynamic Study. Select Random Vibration as the type of dynamic study. Name the study Random Vibration 01.

Copying the **Frequency** study into a **Dynamic Random** study also copies the mesh and restraints information.

The required properties of the **Random Vibration** study are shown in Figure 16-11.

Frequency Options   Random Vibration Options

Figure 16-11: Properties of the Random Vibration study.

The Frequency Options specify all modes in the range of 0-2500Hz to be considered in the analysis of random vibrations. The Frequency Options have been copied from Modal study; you don't have to define them.

In the Random Vibration options, specify the Upper limit as 2500Hz to investigate responses to Random Vibration in the frequency range from 0 to 2500Hz.

Define **Global Damping** as shown in Figure 16-12.

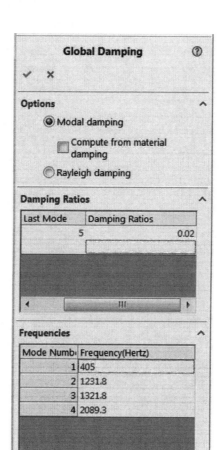

Figure 16-12: Global damping definition.

Global damping is defined as 2% of critical damping. The number of modes is 5; this is a "left-over" from the default choice in Frequency Options. The actual number of frequencies is 4 and corresponds to the number of modes in the frequency range defined in Figure 16-11.

Assigning the same damping ratio to all modes represents a simplified and conservative approach. In most cases damping for higher modes will be higher than for lower modes.

The load on the hard drive head comes from random excitation of the base in the global Y direction. Follow Figure 16-13 to define the Acceleration PSD. The Acceleration PSD has been obtained from testing.

(1) Right-click External Loads select Uniform Base Excitation

(2) Read this message Make selections indicated below

Acceleration PSD

Unit G²/Hz

Along global Y

Select curve Click Edit

(3) Select Hz

Enter the coordinates of four points defining the PSD curve

(4) Click View in the Uniform Base Excitation window to review the PSD curve.

Figure 16-13: Uniform Base Excitation defined as the Acceleration PSD in the global Y direction acting on all restraints present in the model. In our model only one restraint is present.

Follow the above steps to create the Acceleration PSD curve. The graph has been formatted in Excel.

Define two **Sensors** as shown in Figure 16-14.

Figure 16-14: Sensor locations: Two vertices are selected: at the tip of the head and at the end of the fillet.

The above is for information only; the HD HEAD model comes with sensors already defined.

Define **Result Options** as shown in Figure 16-15.

All tracked Data Sensors ———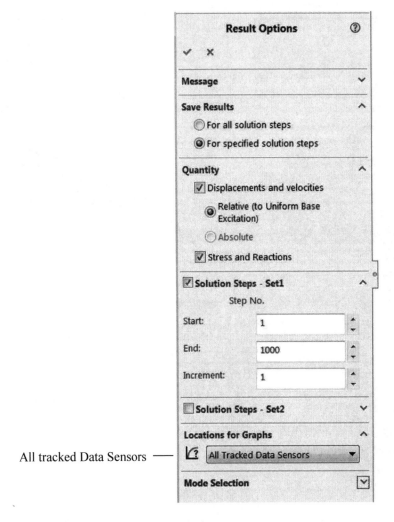

Figure 16-15: Result Options.

All tracked Data Sensors includes the two locations selected in the Sensor definition window in Figure 16-14.

Obtain the solution and analyze the RMS displacement results and the PSD displacement results.

Define UY displacement plot of RMS and PSD displacements as shown in Figure 16-16.

Figure 16-16: RMS displacement results and PSD Absolute Maximum UY displacement component.

The maximum RMS displacement is 0.084mm.The maximum PSD displacement is $0.00026mm^2/Hz$.

PSD displacements are displayed in units of mm^2/Hz for the **Absolute Maximum** found in the frequency range. The **Absolute Maximum** of PSD displacement corresponds to the first mode frequency 405Hz.

It is important to understand the meaning of results in a **Random Vibration** analysis. The displacement results in Figure 16-16 (top) are the RMS displacements. The maximum RMS displacement is 0.084mm meaning that the magnitude of displacement has a 68% probability of remaining under 0.084mm. The probability of the maximum displacement magnitude exceeding 0.084mm is 100% - 68% = 32%.

Remembering that the probability of a given displacement is defined by a normal distribution for which σ = 0.084mm, we can calculate the probability of displacement magnitude exceeding any defined value (Figure 16-17).

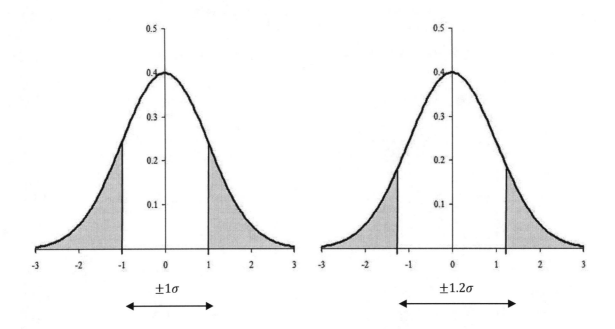

Figure 16-17: The total area under the normalized Gauss curve is 1. The probability of displacement magnitude exceeding ±σ (left) and ±1.2σ (right) is equal to the corresponding shaded areas.

*The probability of the displacement magnitude exceeding 1*RMS displacement, here 0.084mm, is given by the area outside ± 1σ which is 32% (left).*

*The probability of displacement magnitude exceeding 1.2*RMS displacement (0.10mm) is given by the area outside ± 1.2σ which is 23% (right).*

The same applies to all results of a Random Vibration analysis. The RMS von Mises stress result is shown in Figure 16-18.

Stress concentration

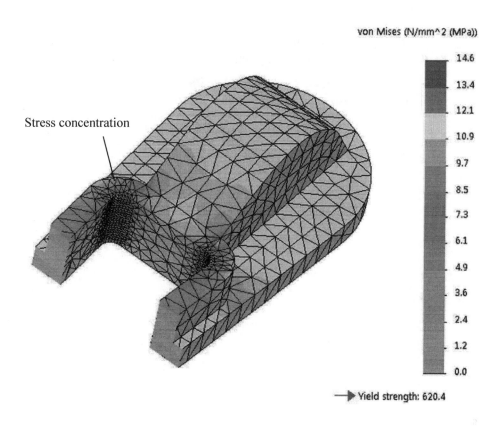

Figure 16-18: RMS von Mises stress plot.

The maximum von Mises stress has a 68% probability of remaining below 14.6MPa. Section Clipping is used in this plot; stress concentrations are present on both sides but are shown on one side only.

Notice that stress singularities present in the model (sharp re-entrant edges) do not show as stress concentrations because of a large element size used for meshing. Refer to Figure 16-18 and compare the size of elements to the size of the stress concentration. Even with mesh controls applied, the mesh is at best marginal to model stress concentrations. Repeat the analysis using a more refined mesh.

The results of **Dynamic Random** analysis presented as RMS values provide one result for the entire frequency range of excitation. Results of Random Vibration analysis such as displacements or stresses may also be presented as PSD values, which are different for each excitation frequency. Examine the PSD options of displacements and stress result plots and notice that displacement results are given in mm^2/Hz, and stress results are given in MPa^2/Hz. These units are a consequence of the base excitation being defined as acceleration squared per frequency range, in our case G_{RMS}^2/Hz.

The most informative way to review PSD results is to graph them over the frequency range. Create two graphs showing PSD displacement of the tip of the head defined by the sensor shown in Figure 16-14. These two graphs are shown in Figure 16-19.

<u>Figure 16-19: PSD UY and UZ displacement components of the tip as a function of excitation frequency in configuration *01 aligned.*</u>

Notice a very different scale of Y axis in UY and UZ response graphs. These graphs have been formatted in Excel.

Modal shapes of mode 1 and mode 3 are aligned with the direction of base excitation. Indeed, upon examination of the UY response graph in Figure 16-19 we see that mode 1 and mode 3 are excited, even though the effect of mode 3 is visible only because a logarithmic scale is used. The UZ response graph does not show any modes excited. The peaks visible on the UZ graph are results of discretization error.

The area under the PSD UY response graph equals the RMS^2 displacement of the vertex where the sensor has been defined. This can be proven by integrating the PSD UY displacement function. If you wish to perform the numerical integration, then for better accuracy copy the study *Random Vibration 01* into *Random Vibration 01 small steps* and use settings shown in Figure 16-20.

50 frequency points

Figure 16-20: Settings of *Random Vibration 01 small steps* study.

Specify 50 frequency points. Four frequencies are found in the 0-2500Hz range. Therefore, with 50 frequency points, the solution will proceed in 251 frequency steps.

Figure 16-21 shows the UY PSD response graph based on 251 frequency steps; it uses a linear scale on the Y axis. See spreadsheet HD HEAD.xlsx for numerical integration results.

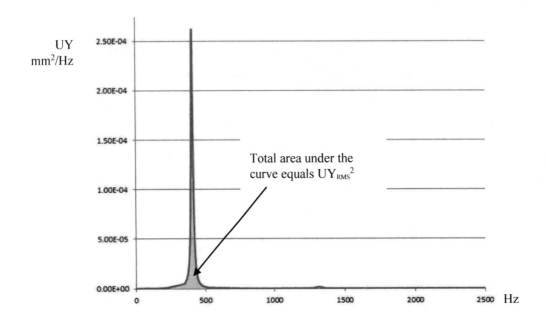

Figure 16-21: Correspondence between RMS and PSD UY displacement: Total area under the curve equals UY_{RMS}^2.

See the spreadsheet HD HEAD.xlsx for details.

Now, change to configuration *02 not aligned*, create a **Random** study titled *Random Vibration 02* and repeat the analysis. Everything except the model position will be identical to study *Random Vibration 01*. Obtain the solution and construct PSD response graphs for UY and UZ displacement components of the tip. These graphs are shown in Figure 16-22 and are directly comparable to the graphs presented in Figure 16-19.

Figure 16-22: PSD UY and UZ displacement components of the tip as a function of excitation frequency in configuration *02 misaligned.*

Four peaks in each graph correspond to the four modes exited by the base excitation.

Upon examination of the graphs in Figure 16-22, we find that in configuration *02 misaligned*, all four modes are excited; this is easiest to show using a logarithmic scale. Mode 1 still dominates the vibration response.

Summary of studies completed

Model	Configuration	Study Name	Study Type
HD HEAD.sldasm	01 aligned	*Modal*	Frequency
		Random Vibration 01	Random Vibration
		Random Vibration 01 small steps	Random Vibration
	02 misaligned	*Random Vibration 02*	Random Vibration

Figure 16-23: Names and types of studies completed in this chapter.

17: Response spectrum analysis

Topics covered

- ❑ Non stationary random base excitation
- ❑ Seismic response analysis
- ❑ Seismic records
- ❑ Response spectrum method
- ❑ Generating response spectra
- ❑ Methods of mode combination

Non stationary excitation

Many random events are not stationary meaning that parameters such as mean or variance do not remain the same but change with time. Important examples of a non-stationary process are earthquake and pyrotechnic shock. Figure 17-1 shows an acceleration time history of an earthquake recorded in California zone 4. The event duration is 31s; considering a sampling rate of 0.005s the curve consists of 6145 data points.

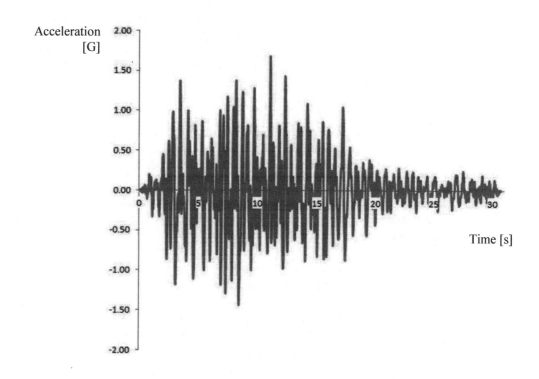

Figure 17-1: An example of acceleration time history of an earthquake.

Source: vibrationdata.com.

The earthquake is a non-stationary process and the methods of Random Vibration analysis cannot be used. At the same time, given the amount of data points, a **Time Response** analysis is impractical. For these reasons, a special analysis method called the **Response Spectrum Method** has been developed to analyze long duration non-stationary processes like the earthquakes or pyrotechnic shock events.

We will explain the concept of the **Response Spectrum Method** in the following steps:

1. A system vibrating in resonance can be described as a single degree of freedom harmonic oscillator system characterized by mass, stiffness and damping.

2. A response of a system with more than one resonant frequency can be represented as a combination of responses of harmonic oscillators, with each harmonic oscillator corresponding to a particular resonant frequency. Notice that this is the basis of the modal superposition method.

3. If the excitation frequency is equal to one of structure's resonance frequencies, then the system response to that excitation is controlled only by system damping. Mass does not matter, stiffness does not matter; they have no impact on the system's response. The **only** thing controlling the system response is its damping!

Imagine that two vastly different systems, a harmonic oscillator and a bridge, have two important things in common: the resonant frequency and damping. Now imagine that both the harmonic oscillator and the bridge are excited by the same excitation that happens to have the same frequency as the resonance frequency of both the harmonic oscillator and the bridge. The vibration response (e.g. the maximum displacement) will be the same for the harmonic oscillator and the bridge!

4. Let's assume that the vibration response can be adequately modeled with the modal superposition method based, for example, on five modes. Using the observations made in point **3.**, we may simplify the analysis very significantly. Rather than studying the response of the actual structure, we can study the response of five harmonic oscillators with natural frequencies corresponding to those five modes and associated damping being the same as the modes and damping of the structure we wish to analyze. In particular, if we study the structure's response to seismic excitation, then rather than testing the actual structure, we can just subject those five oscillators to the earthquake acceleration time history and record the maximum displacement, velocity, and acceleration of each oscillator. Next, we plot the maximum displacement, velocity, and acceleration of each oscillator as a function of the oscillator's frequency. This way a **Response Spectrum** curve is built. The maximum displacement recorded as a function of frequency is the **Displacement Response Spectrum**, the maximum velocity recorded as a function of frequency is the **Velocity Response Spectrum** and the maximum acceleration recorded as a function of frequency is the **Acceleration Response Spectrum**. The above reasoning may be extended to any number of harmonic oscillators.

5. The examined structure does not have to have the same resonant frequencies as our set of harmonic oscillators described in point **4**. If the resonant frequencies of the analyzed structure fall "in-between" frequencies of the oscillators used to construct the **Response Spectrum** curve, the structure response can be interpolated. So if resonant frequencies of the analyzed structures are known and we also know the **Acceleration Response Spectrum** curve that has just been constructed by examining the response of harmonic oscillators, then we can find out by interpolation, the maximum acceleration of the structure corresponding to each mode. Double integration will give the maximum displacement.

6. The information of interactions between modes has been lost in the above process. Therefore, it must be re-built using one of the methods of combining the maximum vibration response of each mode. The commonly used methods are the **Square Root of Sum of Squares** (SRSS) and the **Absolute Sum**. These methods will be described later.

We will expand on point **4**. Figure 17-2 shows a series of Single Degree of Freedom (SDOF) oscillators all attached to a common base. Their natural frequencies are different, changing from the lowest 3Hz to the highest 30Hz. All SDOF oscillators have the same damping ratio. This base is subjected to excitation with the acceleration time history shown in Figure 17-1.

3Hz   10Hz   16Hz   24Hz   30Hz

Figure 17-2: An illustrative explanation of the Response Spectrum concept: a set of five SDOF oscillators is subjected to base excitation with acceleration time history recorded from an earthquake.

The range of frequencies 3-30Hz is divided into four parts: 3-10Hz, 10-16Hz, 16-24Hz, and 24-30Hz.

A **Time Response** analysis of the set of SDOFs in Figure 17-2 is conducted and the maximum absolute displacement, velocity, and acceleration are found for each oscillator. The **Time Response** analysis is easy because of simplicity of this system; it has only five DOFs. The corresponding **Response Spectrum** curves will have five points. An example of an **Acceleration Response Spectrum** curve is shown in Figure 17-3.

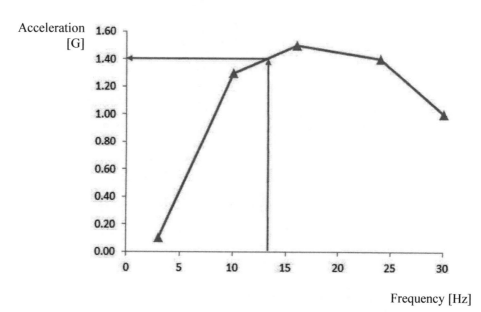

Figure 17-3: An Acceleration Response Spectrum curve generated from the results of a Time Response analysis of a series of SDOFs with frequencies 3Hz, 10Hz, 16Hz, 24Hz, and 30Hz.

The curve serves as an illustrative example only; it does not correspond to any seismic shock.

Response for frequencies falling "in-between" the natural frequencies of the oscillators shown in Figure 17-2 may be interpolated. Figure 17-3 shows a linear interpolation.

Assume for a moment that natural frequencies of a structure are dominated by a single mode and the direction of excitation is aligned with that mode. In this case the response (e.g. maximum acceleration) can be read from a graph. Finite Element Analysis programs merely automate interpolation and combine effects of multiple modes and different excitation directions.

The direction of excitation with regard to the direction of modal shape must be taken into consideration when a **Response Spectrum** curve is constructed. This is illustratively shown in Figure 17-4.

Figure 17-4: Illustrative explanation of the Response Spectrum concept taking into consideration that the direction of excitation and the directions of modal shapes may not be aligned.

Excitation is applied perpendicularly to the base; oscillators are located "at an angle" to the direction of excitation.

Most often the **Response Spectra** curves are produced by subjecting the series of SDOFs to a synthesized acceleration time history that does not correspond to any particular earthquake but represents an earthquake that may happen in a given geographical region. The synthesized **Response Spectra** curves can be found in seismic codes and are used as inputs to seismic analyses. An example of some **Response Spectra** for equipment installed in a building during a seismic event is shown in Figure 17-5.

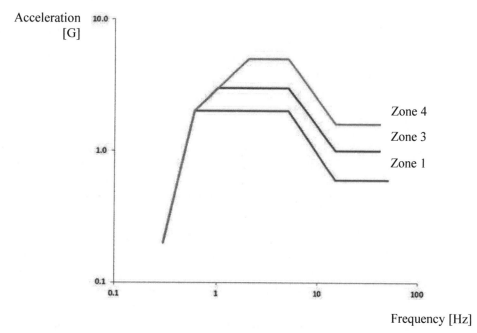

Figure 17-5: Response Spectra for different seismic zones.

For more information see: en.wikipedia.org/wiki/Network_Equipment-Building-System.

The **Response Spectra** shown in Figure 17-5 are not meant to be used as an input to seismic analysis of an entire building. These are accelerations in the horizontal direction of an upper floor of a building during an earthquake.

Even though the **Response Spectrum** method is ubiquitous in earthquake engineering, it has important limitations. Finite Element Analysis programs like **SOLIDWORKS Simulation** calculate the response of each mode independently and then must somehow combine them together. The maximum responses in different modes do not have to coincide in time; therefore, these responses cannot be combined directly. **SOLIDWORKS Simulation** offers a choice of four approximate methods of combining individual modal responses:

Square Root Sum of Squares (SRSS)

Absolute Sum (ABS)

Complete Quadratic Combination (CQC)

Naval Research Laboratory (NRL)

The **SRSS** estimates the peak response by the square root of the sum of the maximum responses squared. The **ABS** method assumes that the maximum modal responses occur at the same time for all modes. This is the most conservative method of modal combination. The **CQC** is based on random vibration concepts, and **NRL** takes the absolute value of the largest response and adds it to the **SRSS** response of other modes.

How many modes should be considered when modeling a structure's response to a seismic shock? Most often seismic analysis is conducted to demonstrate compliance with certain code requirements. That specific code will specify the minimum mass participation factor in the model used for seismic response. Hence, we need to use as many modes as necessary to ensure the required mass participation.

We'll demonstrate the use of **SOLIDWORKS Simulation** for the analysis of a seismic response using the assembly model titled FRAME, shown in Figure 17-6. Base excitation in the form of a **Response Spectrum** will be similar to the Zone 4 excitation in Figure 17-5. Our objective is to analyze displacements and accelerations experienced by the FRAME installed on an upper floor of a building experiencing **Zone 4** seismic shock. Sharp re-entrant edges in the model geometry are acceptable because stress analysis is not an objective of this exercise.

The model consists of a steel cylinder resting on a plastic frame as shown in Figure 17-6.

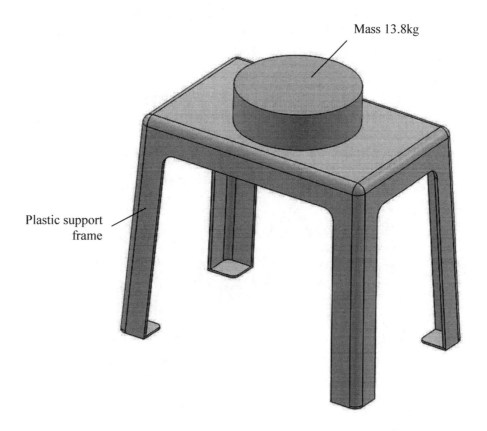

Mass 13.8kg

Plastic support frame

Figure 17-6: The FRAME model used for the analysis of a seismic shock.

All legs have fixed restraints applied to the pads.

Notice the sharp re-entrant edges in the model.

A **Response Spectrum** study does not allow for use of reference geometry in the definition of the direction of excitations. They can be only applied in the global X, Y, or Z directions. Therefore, the assembly model is located "at an angle" with respect to the global coordinate system and excitation will be applied in the X direction (Figure 17-7).

Direction of excitation

Figure 17-7: Location of the FRAME relative to the global coordinate system of the assembly.

Excitation is applied in the X direction of the global coordinate system. The arrow indicates the direction of excitation and the direction of x axis of the global coordinate system.

Prior to the **Response Spectrum** analysis we'll find modes of vibration within the range of frequencies 0-50Hz. Create **Frequency** study *Modal* with default five modes and define **Fixed** restrains to four pads as shown on Figure 17-6. Mesh the assembly with a **Curvature base mesh** with the default element size.

Three modes within the range of 0-50Hz are shown in Figure 17-8.

Mode 1: 19Hz

Mode 2: 20Hz

Mode 3: 48Hz

Figure 17-8: The three modes of vibration of the FRAME within the range of 0-50Hz. Arrows indicate the direction of vibration.

Only Mode 3 is aligned with the global direction; it is aligned with Y axis of the global coordinate system.

The direction of base excitation is along the global X direction; therefore, mode 1 and mode 2 will participate in the vibration response. Mode 3 is orthogonal to the direction of excitation and will not be excited by the applied base excitation. The **Response Spectrum** method uses the **Modal Superposition Method** to find the vibration response; therefore, the vibration response will be a superposition of the responses of mode 1 and mode 2.

Create a **Response Spectrum** study as shown in Figure 17-9, call it *ABS*; we will use the ABS method to combine individual modal responses.

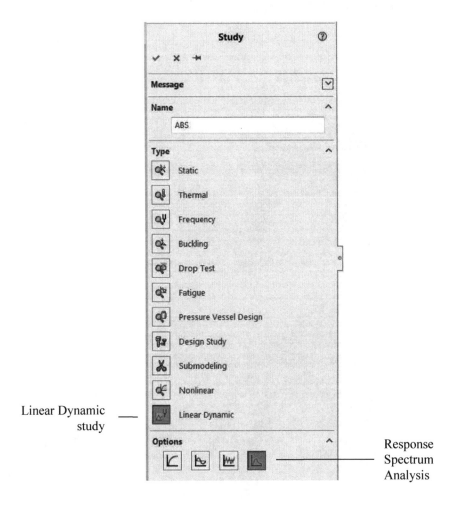

Figure 17-9: Definition of a Linear Dynamic study with the Response Spectrum Analysis option.

Define a **Uniform Base Excitation** as shown in Figure 17-10.

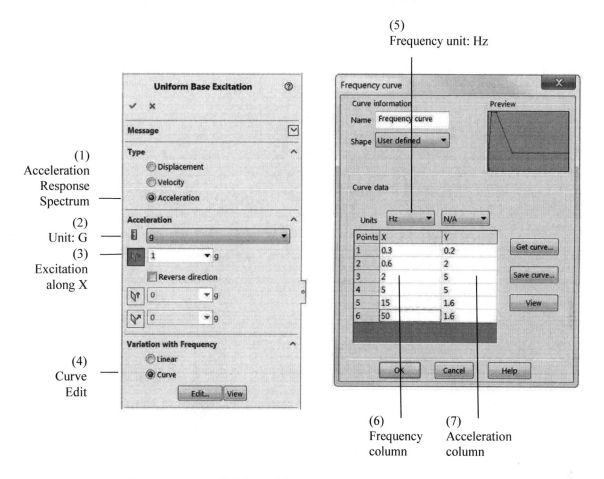

Figure 17-10: Definition of the base excitation.

Numbers in the acceleration column are multipliers to the gravitational acceleration entered in step 3. You may copy the Response Spectrum table from the spreadsheet titled FRAME.xlsx and paste it into the Frequency curve window.

Define restraints as shown in Figure 17-6 and mesh using a **Curvature based mesh** with default settings; the mesh will be same as the one used in Frequency study. It is shown in Figure 17-11.

Figure 17-11: The FRAME assembly after meshing.

A curvature based mesh is recommended because of curvilinear geometry.

Define the study properties as shown in Figure 17-12.

Five frequencies

Absolute Sum method of mode combination

Logarithmic interpolation of Response Spectrum curve

Frequency Options   Response Spectrum Options

Figure 17-12: Response Spectrum Study properties.

Since five frequencies are specified, the first five modes may possibly contribute to the seismic response.

In preparation for a **Response Spectrum** analysis, we conducted a modal analysis. The results of the modal analysis indicated that only the first two modes will participate in the seismic response. Yet, we specify five modes in **Frequency Options**. This is to prove that indeed only the first two modes are important in the seismic response; it will be clearly seen from the modal mass participation results.

Obtain the solution and create a plot of acceleration as shown in Figure 17-13.

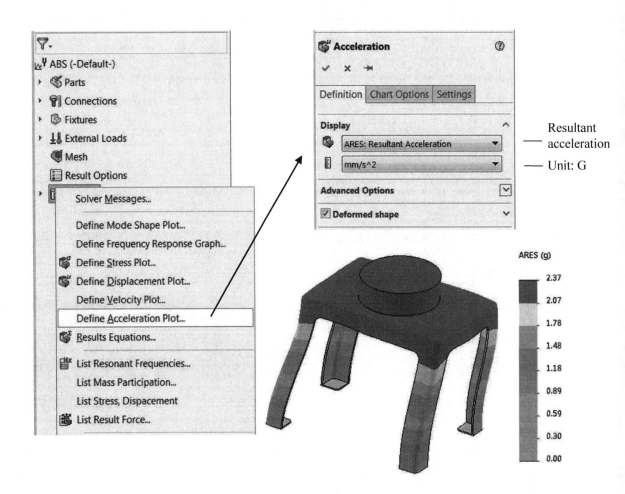

Figure 17-13: The maximum resultant acceleration during the Zone 4 seismic event.

The maximum resultant acceleration relative to the base is 2.37G.

Even though the maximum acceleration plot (as well as other plots) may be animated, the animation has no physical meaning in a **Response Spectrum** study. Remember that the results show the maximum values of acceleration during the entire duration of excitation. It is unknown at which point in time the maximum response happens. Also remember that the maximum response is the result of an arbitrary combination of individual modal responses, here performed using the **ABS** method. The same applies to all results of a **Response Spectrum** analysis.

Create the **Effective mass participation factor** window as shown in Figure 17-14.

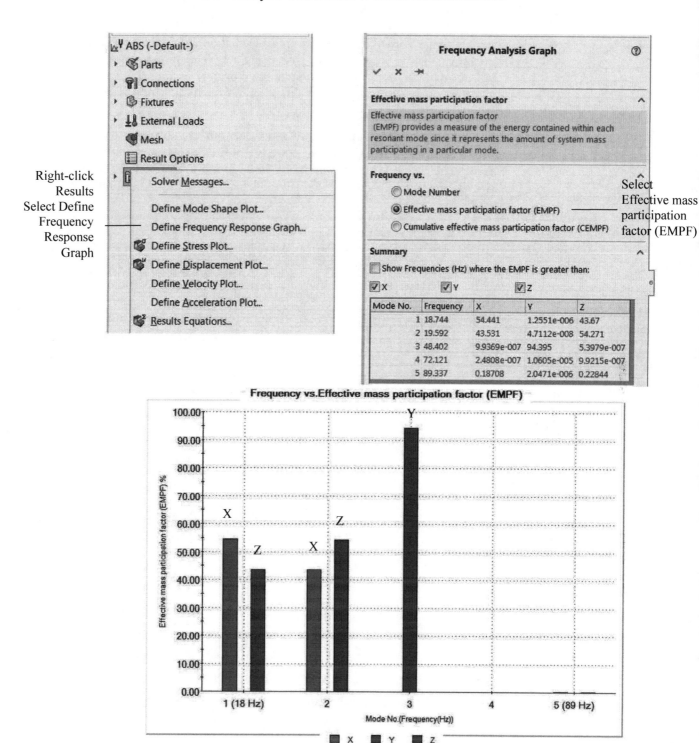

Right-click
Results
Select Define
Frequency
Response
Graph

Select
Effective mass
participation
factor (EMPF)

Figure 17-14: Mass participation of the first five modes; mode 4 and mode 5 do not participate in the response.

Directions X, Y, Z are identified by colors impossible to show in this black and white illustration even with added labels X, Y, Z; review this graph on screen.

A review of the **Mass Participation** indicates that only the first and second modes participate in response to the seismic shock. The third mode with its frequency of 48.3Hz is still within the range of excitation frequencies 0-50Hz, but its direction is orthogonal to the direction of excitation. Modes 4 and 5 have no mass participation in any direction.

To gain a better understanding of how individual modes contribute to the seismic response we will create two more **Response Spectrum** studies: *Seismic shock mode 1* and *Seismic shock mode 2* with **Frequency Options** shown in Figure 17-15. Each study will model a seismic response using only one mode.

Frequency
of mode 1

Frequency
of mode 2

Frequency Options in study
Seismic shock mode 1

Frequency Options in study
Seismic shock mode 2

Figure 17-15: Frequency Options in the two studies used to analyze the individual mode contributions to the seismic response.

Seismic shock mode 1 study is based on the first mode: 18.74Hz.

Seismic shock mode 2 study is based on the second mode: 19.58Hz.

Notice that the **Frequency Options** of study *Seismic shock mode 1* could also be defined by specifying the number of frequencies equal to one. This is because 18.74Hz is the frequency of the first mode. The method of combining individual modal responses is irrelevant in *Seismic shock mode 1* and *Seismic shock mode 2* because each study is based on one mode only.

Results of the three studies *ABS*, *Seismic shock mode 1* and *Seismic Shock mode 2* are shown in Figure 17-16:

Figure 17-16: Acceleration results of studies based on mode 1 and mode 2 (top), and acceleration results based on the five modes out of which only the first two contribute to the response (bottom).

The maximum acceleration based on mode 1 is 1.24G; the maximum acceleration based on mode 2 is 1.12G. The acceleration based on both modes is 2.37G.

The maximum acceleration found in study *ABS* is the **Absolute Sum** of the maximum acceleration in each mode. The difference in the second decimal place is caused by numerical error.

Run three more studies to try other **Mode Combination Methods** available in SOLIDWORKS Simulation:

Study *SRSS*: **Square Root of Squares (SRSS)**

Study *CQC*: **Complete Quadratic Combination (CQC)**

Study *NRL*: **Naval Research Laboratory**.

The summary of results is shown in Figure 17-17.

Square Root
Sum of Squares

Absolute Sum

Complete Quadratic
Combination

Naval Research
Laboratory

Figure 17-17: Acceleration results of study Seismic shock (based on two modes) using different methods of mode combination.

The Absolute Sum is the most conservative method.

Summary of studies completed

Model	Configuration	Study Name	Study Type
FRAME.sldasm	*Default*	*Modal*	Frequency
		ABS	Response Spectrum Analysis
		Seismic shock mode 1	Response Spectrum Analysis
		Seismic shock mode 2	Response Spectrum Analysis
		SRSS	Response Spectrum Analysis
		CQC	Response Spectrum Analysis
		NRL	Response Spectrum Analysis

Figure 17-18: Names and types of studies completed in this chapter.

18: Nonlinear vibration

Topics covered

- ❑ Differences between linear and nonlinear structural analysis
- ❑ Types of nonlinearities
- ❑ Bending stiffness
- ❑ Membrane stiffness
- ❑ Modal damping
- ❑ Rayleigh damping
- ❑ Linear Time response analysis
- ❑ Nonlinear Time response analysis
- ❑ Modal Superposition Method
- ❑ Direct Integration Method

Difference between linear and nonlinear structural analysis

A structural analysis problem, be it static or time dependent, is always concerned with stiffness of the analyzed structure. If stiffness remains constant during the process of load application then the problem is linear. If stiffness changes then the problem is nonlinear. Nonlinear analyses are classified into different types based on the origin of the nonlinear behavior. For example, in nonlinear geometry analysis stiffness changes because of changes to a structure's geometry, in nonlinear material analysis stiffness changes because of changes in material properties etc. There are many other types of nonlinear analyses. For more information refer to "**Engineering Analysis with SOLIDWORKS Simulation.**"

The nonlinearity in the problems analyzed in this chapter is geometric; it is caused by changes in the structure's shape and requires **Large displacement** analysis. However, the term **Large displacement** is incorrect because it implies that displacements must be large in order for the nonlinear effects to show up even though in many cases small displacements are sufficient to change the stiffness significantly.

Bending and membrane stiffness

Consider a beam represented by the model PLANK, supported on both sides by hinges and subjected to 1MPa pressure as shown in Figure 18-1. The beam material is Alloy Steel, with a thickness of 25.4mm (1").

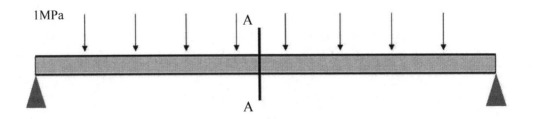

Figure 18-1: A flat beam simply supported on both ends.

The two hinges supporting the beam can't move in any direction.

The stress distribution across the beam thickness in the cross section A-A changes as the beam deformation progresses (Figure 18-2).

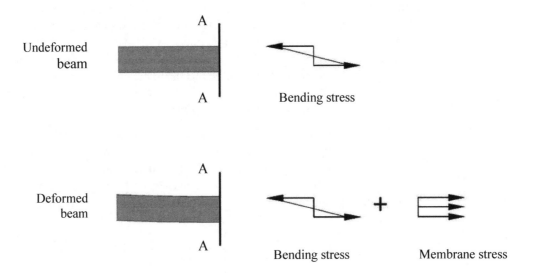

Figure 18-2: Bending stress distribution in cross section A-A in the undeformed beam (top) and in the deformed beam (bottom).

The flat beam responds to load only with bending stress. The curved beam responds to load with bending stress and with tensile stress called membrane stress. Notice that membrane stiffness wouldn't come into existence if one of the supports shown in Figure 18-1 could slide in the horizontal direction.

When the load is first applied and the beam is still flat, the beam can respond only with bending stresses. We may say it only has bending stiffness. As deformation progresses and the beam becomes curved, tensile stresses develop and the beam acquires a new type of stiffness: membrane stiffness. The name "membrane" comes from the analysis of very thin walls called membranes where bending stiffness is negligible and all stiffness is generated by membrane stress. In our case, the stiffness of the curved beam is a superposition of bending and membrane stiffness.

The PLANK model has two configurations: *01 solid* and *02 surface*. We'll use *02 surface* which allows for meshing with shell elements.

A static analysis accounting for nonlinear effects requires either a **Static** study with the **Large displacements** option, or a **Nonlinear** study with the **Large displacements** option. We'll use **Static** studies.

Set up and run two **Static** studies: a linear analysis titled *01 static LIN* and a nonlinear static analysis titled *02 static NL*. To create the nonlinear analysis *02 static NL* you may copy *01 static LIN* into *02 static NL* and select **Large displacements** in the study properties. Remember to define restraints as **Immovable** (not **Fixed**) to model hinge supports on both sides. Contrary to solid elements, this is because shell elements differentiate between these two types of restraints.

Figure 18-3 shows the comparison of displacement results obtained with a **Static** study with and without the **Large displacement** option.

<u>Figure 18-3: Comparison of displacement results of the PLANK treated as linear (top) and nonlinear (bottom) problem.</u>

The scale of deformation (1:1) is the same in both plots.

As can be seen in Figure 18-3, the linear solution ignores the stiffening effect of membrane stresses. Consequently, it severely underestimates the stiffness. Having reviewed displacement results, compare von Mises stress results and notice that the linear analysis produces stresses above yield and the nonlinear analysis produces stresses below yield (Figure 18-4).

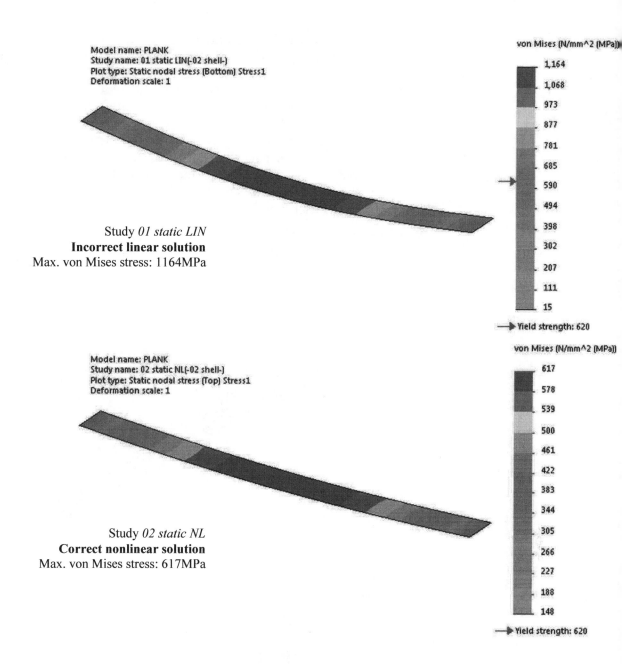

Study *01 static LIN*
Incorrect linear solution
Max. von Mises stress: 1164MPa

Study *02 static NL*
Correct nonlinear solution
Max. von Mises stress: 617MPa

Figure 18-4: Comparison of von Mises stress results of the PLANK treated as linear (top) and nonlinear (bottom).

The scale of deformation (1:1) is the same in both plots. Stress results on the Top of shell elements are shown. The top of elements is the side opposite to where pressure is applied. Review the results on the bottom side. Notice that the linear analysis produces the same von Mises stress on both sides while the nonlinear analysis produces a much higher stress on the top side. This is the effect of membrane stress present in nonlinear analysis.

After this short review explaining the nonlinear nature of the PLANK problem, we move on to the analysis of vibration which will include nonlinear vibration response. This type of analysis is computationally demanding; this is why we use the PLANK model in the *02 surface* configuration suitable for meshing with shell elements. The use of shell elements reduces the solution time significantly. To reduce the solution time even more, use shell elements with a size of 20mm. Large elements are acceptable because the stress distribution across the shell element thickness is built into the element definition and is not dependent on the element size. Furthermore, the overall model stiffness is weakly dependent on the element size. You may want to confirm this by running the same problem with several meshes using different element sizes.

Set up a **Frequency** study titled *03 modal* to find the first two modes of vibration. Again, remember to define **Immovable** (not **Fixed**) restraints. Results of the modal analysis are shown in Figure 18-5.

Mode 1: 60Hz

Mode 2: 241Hz

Figure 18-5: Results of modal analysis.

The first two modes are shown. The rotation on both ends is enabled by hinge restraints.

Notice that modal analysis works with the initial stiffness; it does not take into consideration the membrane stiffening effect.

Having found the modes of vibration, we proceed with a linear **Time Response** analysis available in a **Linear Dynamic** study with the **Modal Time History** option. We already know that the problem is nonlinear. The results of the linear **Time Response** will serve only as a comparison to the results of the subsequent nonlinear **Time Response** analysis.

In the **Modal Time History** study, the PLANK model will be subjected to an impulse pressure shown in Figure 18-6.

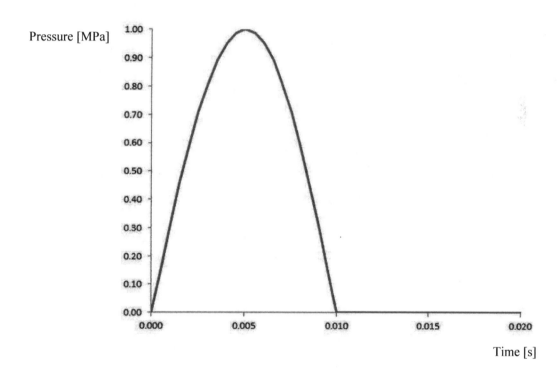

Figure 18-6: Time history of pressure acting on the top face of the PLANK.

During the first 0.01s, pressure rises from zero to 1MPa and drops back to zero. It remains zero until the end of the analysis. The frequency of the sine wave is 50Hz.

Define a **Modal Time History** study titled *04 dynamic LIN* with properties shown in Figure 18-7.

Frequency Options   Dynamic Options

Figure 18-7: Properties of the Modal Time History study.

The study is based on two modes; its duration is 0.2s with a time step of 0.001s.

Define modal damping individually for each mode (Figure 18-8).

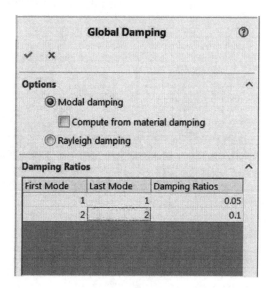

Mode 1: damping 5%
Mode 2: damping 10%

Figure 18-8: Modal damping definition.

Modal damping is defined individually for each mode. We assume these values are known from testing.

Following the definition of the study properties (Figure 18-7), the **Modal Time History** study is based on the superposition of the responses of two modes, each one with different modal damping (Figure 18-8).

Apply a 1MPa pressure to the top face (Figure 18-1); the same as in a static analysis and make it time dependent as shown in Figure 18-9.

(3)
Select User Defined

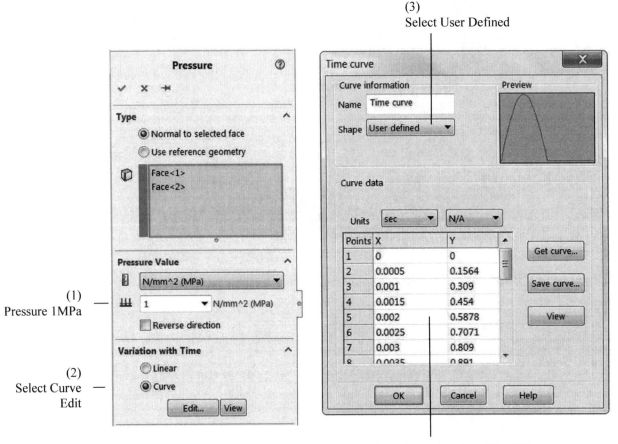

(1)
Pressure 1MPa

(2)
Select Curve
Edit

(4) Paste here table from PLANK.xlsx

Figure 18-9: Definition of time dependent load.

Copy the table from the spreadsheet titled "PLANK.xlsx" into the Time Curve definition window. The table lists the time dependent multiplier to the specified pressure magnitude 1MPa.

Notice that the time duration in the table copied from PLANK.xlsx is only 0.02s, the same as shown in Figure 18-6. The analysis duration specified in the study properties shown in Figure 18-6 is 0.2s. The program will extrapolate the time curve as zero from 0.02s to 0.2s.

Define **Immovable** restraints identical to the previously completed studies. Define **Results Options** as shown in Figure 18-10.

Figure 18-10: Definition of Result Options.

Select the Workflow Sensitive sensor which has been defined in the SOLIDWORKS model.

The study is now ready to run. Obtain the solution and notice that it solves very quickly because it is a linear analysis, and as such, it is based on the **Modal Superposition Method**.

Construct a graph of displacement time history in the mid-span, where the **Workflow Sensitive** sensor has been defined (Figure 18-11).

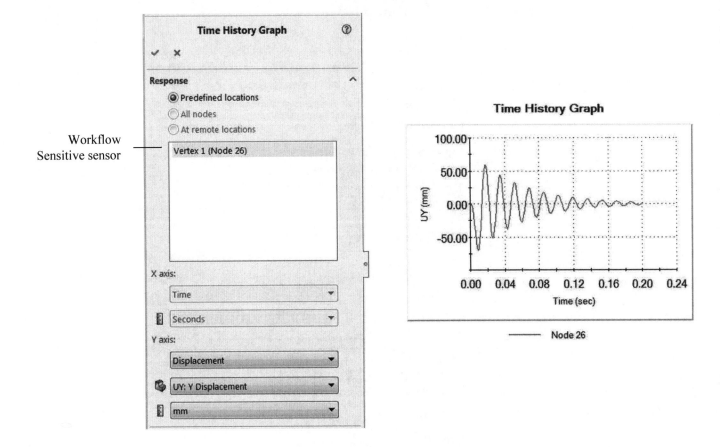

Figure 18-11: Displacement time history in the middle of the beam span.

Select the Workflow Sensitive sensor which has been defined in the SOLIDWORKS model; select the UY displacement component.

Time history of in-plane stress SX will be discussed together with the results of nonlinear analysis.

Notice that when the impulse load disappears after 0.02s the beam performs free damped vibration behaving as a single degree of freedom oscillator. Even though the **Modal Time History** study is based on two modes, the first mode dominates the vibration response.

Previously completed static analysis of this model indicated the importance of nonlinear effects. The nonlinear effects are also present in the vibration response. As we'll soon demonstrate, the above linear solution is incorrect.

We will now perform analysis of the nonlinear vibration response starting with a comparison of the number of Degrees of Freedom (DOF) in the linear and nonlinear vibration problems. The linear vibration problem uses the **Modal Superposition Method**. Two modes have been specified in the study properties; therefore, the problem is represented by two DOFs. The nonlinear problem can't use the **Modal Superposition Method** and must solve all equations of motion in terms of all degrees of freedom present in the model using the **Direct Integration** method.

Look up the **Solver Message** in any of the completed studies to see that the number of DOFs in the model is 6408 (Figure 18-12).

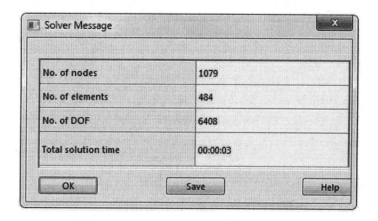

Figure 18-12: The number of DOFs in the PLANK model.

The number of DOFs in the model is 6408. It is not equal to the number of nodes multiplied by six because some DOFs are removed by the restraints.

The comparison between 2 DOFs in the linear problem and the 6408 DOFs in the nonlinear problem gives us an idea how numerically intensive the nonlinear vibration problem will be. This is why the PLANK model is so simple; otherwise it wouldn't solve reasonably fast.

Another consequence of the inability to use the **Modal Superposition Method** is that we can't use modal damping. Damping in nonlinear problems must be defined as **Rayleigh damping**. **Rayleigh damping** makes an arbitrary assumption that the damping matrix is a linear combination of the mass and stiffness matrices. This assumption is a mathematical convenience for the purpose of simplification since there is no physical justification for this. **Rayleigh Damping** is specified by two damping constants: α and β, which are used as multipliers of the mass matrix M and the stiffness matrix K when calculating damping matrix C:

$$[C] = \alpha[M] + \beta[K] \qquad \text{(Eq. 18-1)}$$

$$\frac{\alpha}{2\omega} + \frac{\beta\omega}{2} = \zeta \qquad \text{(Eq. 18-2)}$$

where ω is the frequency and ζ is the damping ratio.

Alpha damping α is a viscous damping component also known as mass damping. It characterizes damping of lower frequencies.

Beta damping β is a hysteresis damping component also known as solid or stiffness damping. It characterizes damping of higher frequencies.

Rayleigh damping components α and β can be found if two modes and their modal damping are known. In our case:

	Frequency Hz	Frequency rad/s	Modal damping %
Mode 1	60	378	5
Mode 2	241	1513	10

Figure 18-13: Modal frequencies and their damping ratios in the PLANK model.

We need to know the above values to find Rayleigh damping.

Using the data in the above table, α and β can be found by solving two equations:

$$\frac{\alpha}{2\omega_1} + \frac{\beta\omega_1}{2} = \zeta_1 \qquad \frac{\alpha}{2\omega_2} + \frac{\beta\omega_2}{2} = \zeta_2 \qquad \text{(Eq. 18-3)}$$

You may also use the spreadsheet "PLANK PAYLEIGH.xlsx" to find $\alpha = 20.17$ and $\beta = 0.00012$.

Knowing α and β, equation (18-2) may be plotted to visualize how damping coefficients change with frequency.

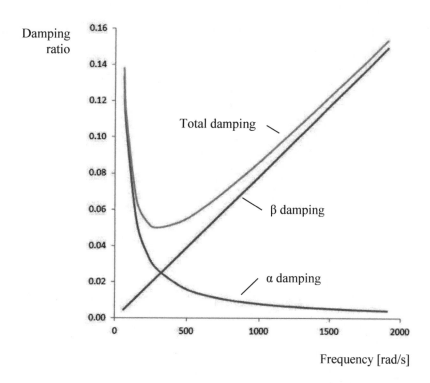

Figure 18-14: Damping ratio and its components as a function of frequency.

α damping drops with frequency; β damping is a linear function of frequency.

The graph in Figure 18-14 serves only to show the importance of **Alfa Damping** and **Beta Damping** for different frequencies; the total damping is not used in solving nonlinear vibration problems. The components α and β are used to formulate damping matrix C, as shown in equation (18-1).

Create a **Nonlinear** study titled *05 dynamic NL* with the **Dynamic** option (Figure 18-15):

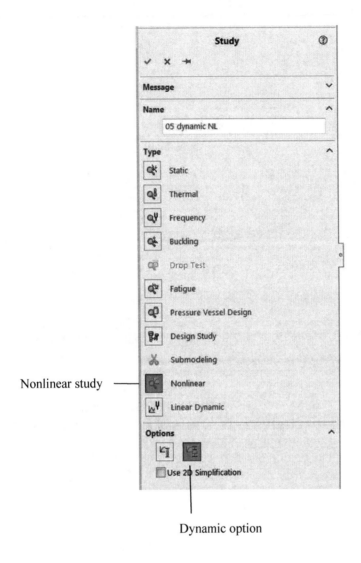

Dynamic option

Figure 18-15: Definition of a Nonlinear study with the Dynamic option.

Define damping as shown in Figure 18-16:

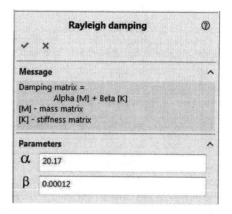

Figure 18-16: Definition of damping in a nonlinear vibration problem.

Enter the previously calculated constants α and β.

Apply the pressure load as a function of time the same way as defined in the linear study. Apply the restraints and use the mesh size the same as well.

We are now ready to define the properties of the nonlinear vibration study as shown in Figure 18-17:

End time 0.2s ——

Auto stepping with
initial time increment
0.002s ——

Large displacement ——

Figure 18-17: Properties of the nonlinear vibration study.

Specify the analysis duration as 0.2s, accept the default auto stepping; select Large displacement.

Large Displacements must be specified or else the problem would not be nonlinear and membrane stiffening would not be accounted for.

Run the solution and acknowledge the warning message produced by the nonlinear solver (Figure 18-18).

Figure 18-18: A warning message of the nonlinear solver issued when the duration of load is shorter than the duration of analysis.

The load duration is 0.02s, analysis duration is 0.2s. The end value of load is zero; therefore, the extrapolated load will be zero for the remaining 0.18s.

Obtain the nonlinear solution and construct displacement and stress graphs the same as in the linear study.

Displacement responses for the linear and nonlinear solution are summarized in Figure 18-19.

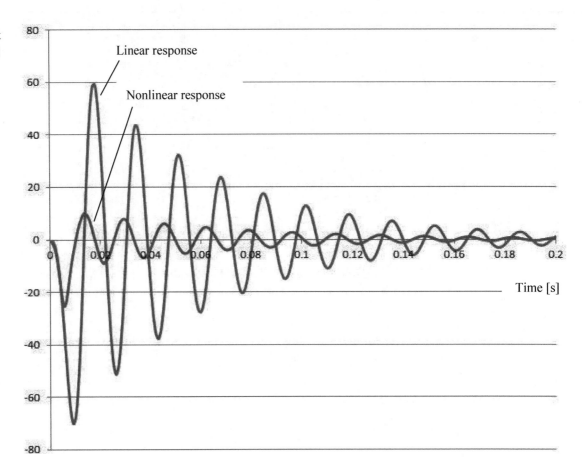

Figure 18-19: Comparison of linear and nonlinear UY displacement results in the mid-span of the PLANK.

The linear response doesn't account for membrane stiffening and produces displacement results with ~300% error.

The comparison between SX stress in the linear and nonlinear solutions in the sensor location is shown in Figure 18-20.

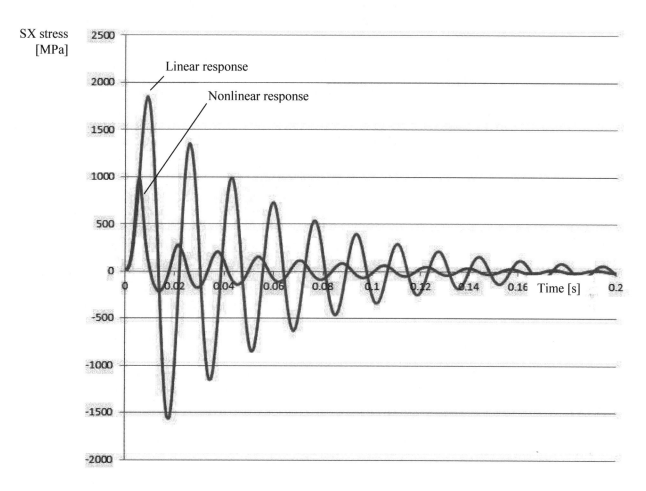

Figure 18-20: Comparison between linear and nonlinear SX stress results in the mid-span of the PLANK.

In the nonlinear response, the magnitude of tensile stress (positive) is larger than the magnitude of compressive stress (negative). This is due to the fact that the sensor location is on the top of the shell elements and does not change location from top to bottom with the reversal of beam deformation.

The frequency of the load time history (50Hz) is close to the first natural frequency of the model; this is the reason for high displacement and stress in the first cycle. Notice that SX stress exceeds the yield strength of the PLANK material (620MPa) in the first vibration cycle indicating that PLANK will experience yield. Whether or not this will result in a structural failure would require an analysis that includes a nonlinear material model.

Different magnitudes of tensile and compressive stresses in the nonlinear SX stress response (Figure 18-20) prove that the nonlinear solution accounts for membrane (tensile) stresses. Remember that all results presented above are reported at the sensor location shown in Figure 18-21.

Figure 18-21: Sensor definition and its importance in the interpretation of results.

The sensor is defined at the end of a split line in the mid-span on the PLANK. Pressure symbols are shown; Immovable restraints symbols are hidden.

Review the shell element orientation (bottoms are orange) to confirm that the top of the PLANK (the side where pressure is applied) has been meshed with the bottoms of shell elements (Figure 18-22).

Figure 18-22: The sensor defined for the shells refers to the top of the shell element. The shell element model has no physical thickness.

The location of the sensor does not differentiate between the top and bottom of the model.

The sensor reads stress at the top of elements (which is the bottom of PLANK) and its location does not change with the reversal of beam deformation. This explains the different magnitudes of tensile and compressive stress in the nonlinear SX time response observed in Figure 18-20.

Summary of studies completed

Model	Configuration	Study Name	Study Type
PLANK.sldprt	*02 surface*	*01 static LIN*	Static
		02 static NL	Static
		03 modal	Frequency
		04 dynamic LIN	Modal Time History
		05 dynamic NL	Nonlinear with Dynamic Option

Figure 18-23: Names and types of studies completed in this chapter.

19: Vibration benchmarks

A benchmark is a standard point of reference against which things may be compared or assessed. In vibration analysis these benchmarks are known as analytical solutions. Solutions of commercial FEA programs may be compared to those known solutions to assess a program's performance.

A large number of vibration benchmarks are available. In this chapter we solve several NAFEMS benchmarks to see how well our results match those benchmark targets.

Since you are already well familiar with all types of vibration analyses with **SOLIDWORKS Simulation**, we'll take shortcuts discussing the setup of these benchmark problems. In some cases the same model will be used for more than one benchmark test and studies will be created in different model configurations.

Because of the number of models, studies, and configurations we present the summary now (Figure 19-1), rather than at the end of the chapter.

Benchmark test	SW model	Configuration	Study name	Study type
NAFEMS test FV2	NAFEMS TEST FV2	01 solids	01 solids	Frequency
		02 shells	02 shells	Frequency
		03 beams	03 beams	Frequency
NAFEMS test 5	NAFEMS TEST 5	01 solids	TEST 5 solids	Harmonic limited to Frequency
		02 shells	TEST 5 shells	Harmonic limited to Frequency
		03 beams	TEST 5 beams	Harmonic limited to Frequency
NAFEMS test 5H	NAFEMS TEST 5	01 solids	TEST 5 solids	Harmonic
		02 shells	TEST 5 shells	Harmonic
		03 beams	TEST 5 beams	Harmonic
NAFEMS test 5T	NAFEMS TEST 5	03 beams	TEST 5T	Modal Time History
		03 beams	TEST 5T 1s	Modal Time History
NAFEMS test 13	NAFEMS TEST 13	Default	TEST 13	Frequency
NAFEMS test 13R	NAFEMS TEST 13	Default	TEST 13R	Random

Figure 19-1: Summary of NAFEMS Benchmark test, corresponding SOLIDWORKS models, model configurations, study names and study types.

NAFEMS test FV2

Pin-ended double cross: in-plane vibration.

Figure 19-2: NAFEMS benchmark test FV2.

Material properties require custom material definition.

Open part model NAFEMS TEST FV2 and review its geometry: eight beams 5m long form a double cross; the beam cross section is a square with side length 0.125m. Material property: E=200000MPa, G=76923MPa, ν=0.3, ρ = 8000kg/m^3. All beams are pin supported at the ends (Figure 19-2).

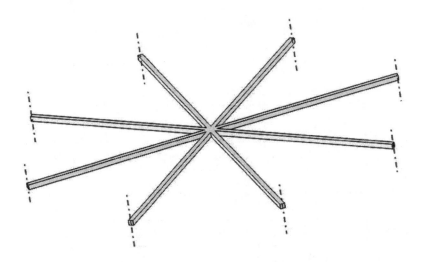

Figure 19-3: Geometry of the double cross model in NAFEMS FV2 shown in the *01solids* configuration.

Pin supports allow for rotation of each end about its own axis. The axes are shown as dotted lines.

Notice that the model geometry lends itself to different representations: volume (solid) geometry for meshing with solid elements, surface geometry for meshing with shell elements and curve (wireframe) geometry for meshing with beam elements. You'll find these three representations in configurations *01 solids*, *02 shells*, and *03 beams*. All configurations have the same custom material with properties specified in the NAFEMS test.

We'll test the model to see how well our results match the benchmark target frequency of 11.336Hz of the first mode. In each configuration create a **Frequency** study with the same name as the configuration name.

Therefore, we'll have to apply proper restraints to make sure that the first mode of vibration will be in-plane and corresponds to what is required in this benchmark test. Notice that 2D option is not available in **Frequency** study.

Change to *01 solids* configuration, create a **Frequency** study and define the restraints for the solid element model as shown in Figure 19-4.

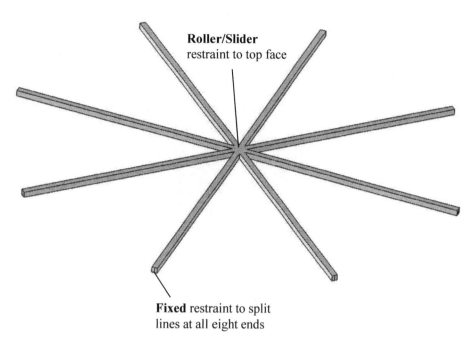

Roller/Slider
restraint to top face

Fixed restraint to split
lines at all eight ends

Figure 19-4: Restraints to the model in the *01 solids* study.

Restraints symbols are not shown. Roller/slide support may be applied to either top face, bottom face or to both.

Remember that nodes of solid elements have three degrees of freedom and can't generate moment reactions. Therefore, **Fixed** restraints to a straight line produce hinges. The **Roller/Slider** restraint eliminates out of plane modes to produce in-plane vibration as required by the test.

Use the default element size to mesh this model and run the solution.

Change to the *02 shells* configurations, create a **Frequency** study and define restraints for the shell element model as shown in Figure 19-5. To apply pin supports, use **Immovable** restraints. To apply restraints enforcing 2D vibration, use **Use Reference Geometry** restraints.

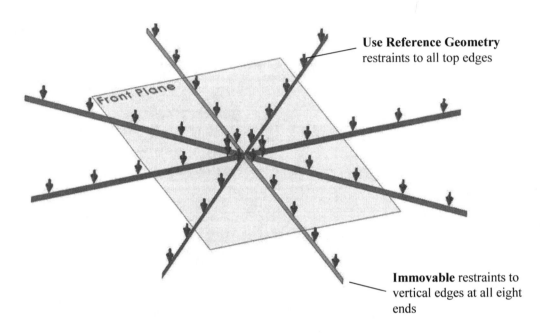

Use Reference Geometry restraints to all top edges

Immovable restraints to vertical edges at all eight ends

Figure 19-5: Restraints to the model in the *02 shells* study.

The Use Reference Geometry support may be applied to either top or bottom face or to both. Immovable restraint symbols are not shown.

The **Immovable** restraints do not affect rotational degrees of freedom of the shell elements and allow for rotation. **Use Reference Geometry** restraints use the **Front Plane** for reference and eliminate translations in the direction normal to this plane. This is necessary to eliminate out of plane modes of vibration. These restraints may be applied to either top or bottom edges.

Define the shell element thickness as 125mm, use the default element size to mesh this model and run the solution.

Change to the *03 beams* configuration. The model geometry is visually identical to the model in the *03 solids* configuration but the eight beams are not merged into one solid body; the model has eight solid bodies. Create a **Frequency** study and change all solid bodies to beams (right-click each solid body and select **Treat as Beam**); calculate joints using **Edit Joints**; define restraints for beam elements as shown in Figure 19-6.

Restraints to eight peripheral joints

Restraint to one central joint

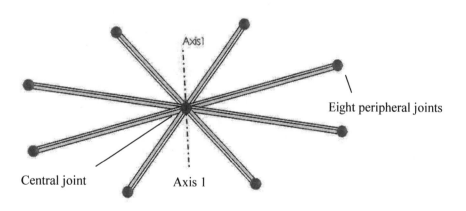

Central joint   Axis 1

Eight peripheral joints

Figure 19-6: Restraints to peripheral joints and to the central joint in the *03 beams* study.

Restraints to the peripheral joints and restraints to the central joint are defined in the cylindrical coordinate system associated with Axis1. Restraint symbols are not shown.

In the peripheral joints shown in Figure 19-6 (left), only rotation in the direction parallel to *Axis1* is allowed; this defines pin supports and eliminates out of plane motions. The central joint has axial translation restrained shown in Figure 19-6 (right) to eliminate lower out of plane modes. Higher out of plane modes are still possible but for us they are irrelevant. All we want to find is the first mode of vibration to see how well the results of **SOLIDWORKS Simulation** match the benchmark target of 11.336Hz.

Results of all three studies are summarized in Figure 19-7.

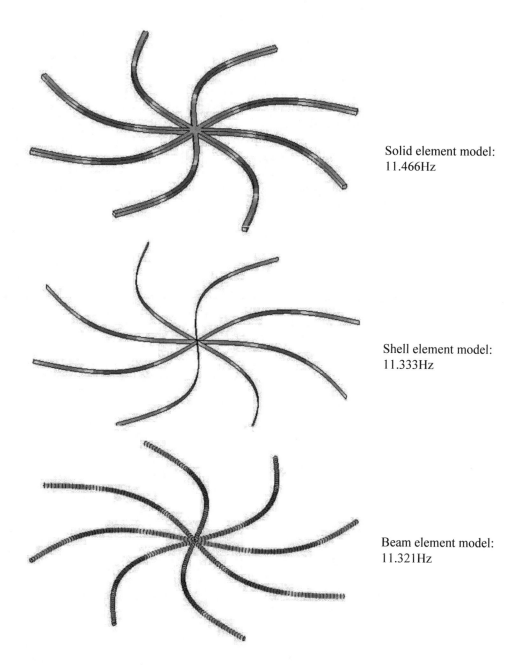

Solid element model: 11.466Hz

Shell element model: 11.333Hz

Beam element model: 11.321Hz

Figure 19-7: First mode of vibration of solid, shell, and beam models.

All shapes correspond to the same first mode of vibration which is an in-plane mode.

All results closely match the exact solution of 11.336Hz.

NAFEMS test 5

Deep Simply-Supported Beam.

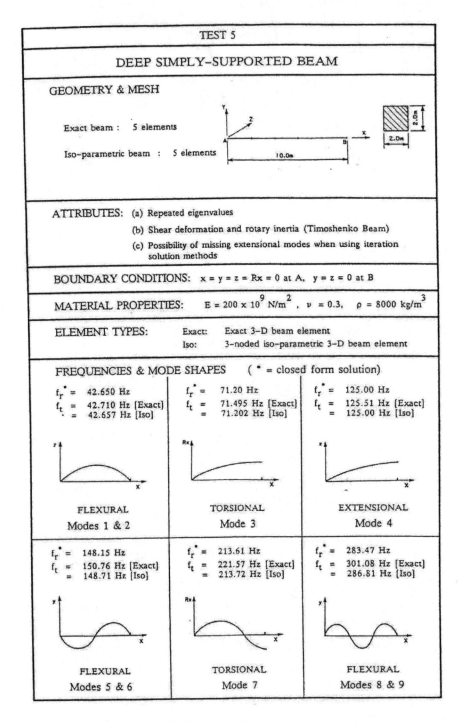

Figure 19-8: NAFEMS TEST 5; Deep Simply-Supported beam.

Custom material properties are the same as in test FV2.

Open part the model NAFEMS TEST 5 and review its geometry: the beam is 10m long, the beam cross section is square with a side length of 2m; the material property is: E = 200000MPa, ρ = 8000kg/m³. The beam has simple supports on both ends (Figure 19-9).

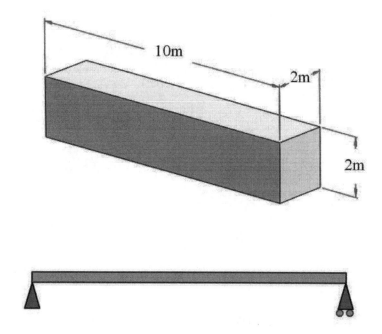

Figure 19-9: Deep Simply-Supported Beam, NAFEMS TEST 5.

Supports are shown schematically in the lower illustration.

We'll test the model to see how well the results match the benchmark target frequency of 42.65Hz in the first mode. The model geometry lends itself to different representations: volume (solid) geometry for meshing with solid elements, surface geometry for meshing with shell elements, and curve (wireframe) geometry for meshing with beam elements. You'll find these different representations in configurations *01 solids*, *02 shells*, and *03 beams*. In each configuration create a **Harmonic** study with names corresponding to names of the configurations: *TEST 5 solids, TEST 5 shells,* and *TEST 5 beams.* Why are we creating **Harmonic** studies rather than **Frequency** studies? Modal analysis can be conducted in both **Frequency** and **Harmonic** studies. Once we complete NAFEMS TEST 5 we'll continue with NAFEMS TEST 5H which does require a **Harmonic** analysis and we'll use the same studies for both tests.

Review the sensors defined in each configuration named *01 Solids*, *02 Shells*, and *03 Beams*. Notice that split lines are used to locate the sensors.

Change to the *01 Solids* configuration, create a **Harmonic** study titled *TEST 5 solids* and define restraints for the solid element model as shown in Figure 19-10.

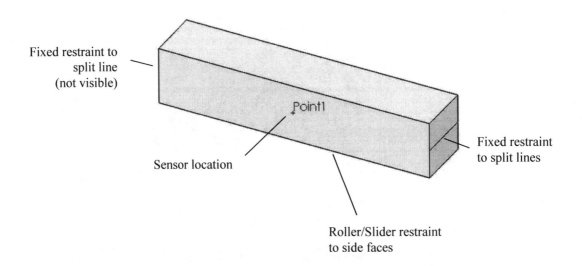

Figure 19-10: Restraints of the model in the *TEST 5 solids* study.

The Fixed restraint applied to a straight edge of a solid model defines a hinge restraint. The Roller/Slider restraints eliminates out of plane modes. Restraints symbols are not shown. Sensor is located in the Reference Point.

Notice that modal analysis is based on the assumption of linearity and that displacements are considered small. Therefore, modal analysis can't distinguish between a sliding and fixed support shown in Figure 19-11. Refer to "Engineering Analysis with SOLIDWORKS Simulation" Chapter 14 for more information.

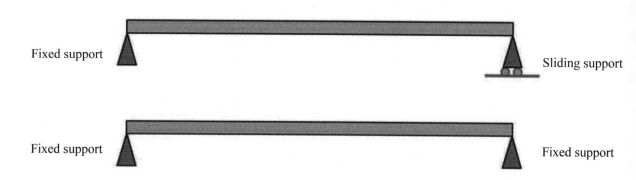

Figure 19-11: Simply supported beam with one fixed and one sliding support (top) and with both supports fixed (bottom). Modal analysis does not distinguish between these two configurations.

The top configuration is statically determinable; the bottom configuration is statically undeterminable.

Change to the *02 shells* configuration, create a **Harmonic** study titled *TEST 5 shells* and define restraints for shell element model as shown in Figure 19-12.

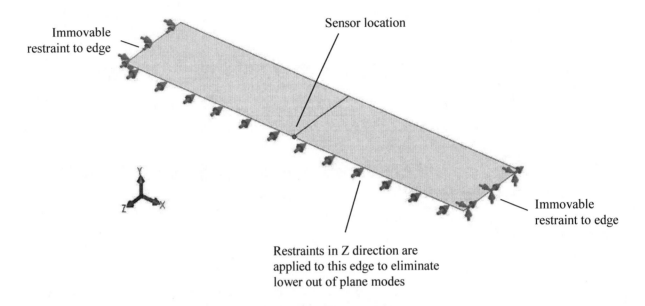

Figure 19-12: Restraints in the model in the *TEST 5 shells* study.

The shell element model does differentiate between Immovable and Fixed restraints. Use Immovable to define a simple support.

In the **Shell Definition**, enter a shell element thickness of 2m and select the **Thick** shell formulation (Figure 19-13).

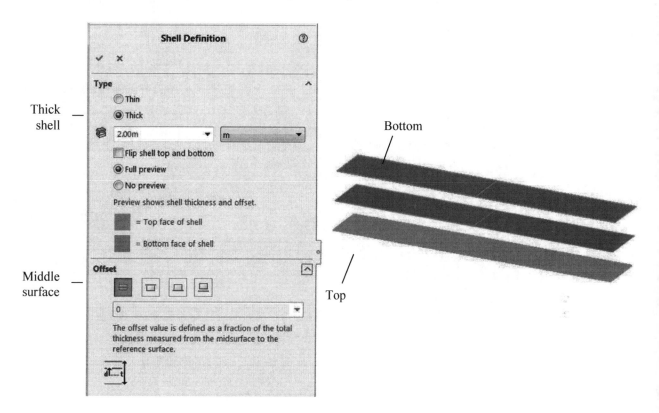

Figure 19-13: The Shell Definition uses the Thick shell formulation.

Select Middle surface for symmetric placement of thickness. Thickness is placed symmetrically.

Change to the *03 beams* configuration and create a **Harmonic** study titled *TEST 5 beams*. Instruct **Simulation** to treat both solid bodies as beams; ignore the warning that the beams are too short. This will have no effect on the results produced by the beam element model. Define restraints for the beam element model as shown in Figure 19-14.

Left joint only — Joint<1, 1>

Front Plane

Restraint to the left joint eliminates rotation about the x and y axes.

Left and right joints

Restraints to both joints eliminate all translations

Left joint:
All translations eliminated;
Rotation about x and y axes eliminated.

Right joint:
All translations eliminated

Figure 19-14: Restraints of the model in the *TEST 5 beams* study.

Immovable restraints to both sides leave the model with one Rigid Body Motion. This is why we need to restrain the model from rotation.

We have defined all three studies to the point where modal analysis can be run. Use the default mesh in all studies. Use **Run Frequency** to obtain modal solution of the above three studies.

Results are summarized in Figure 19-15.

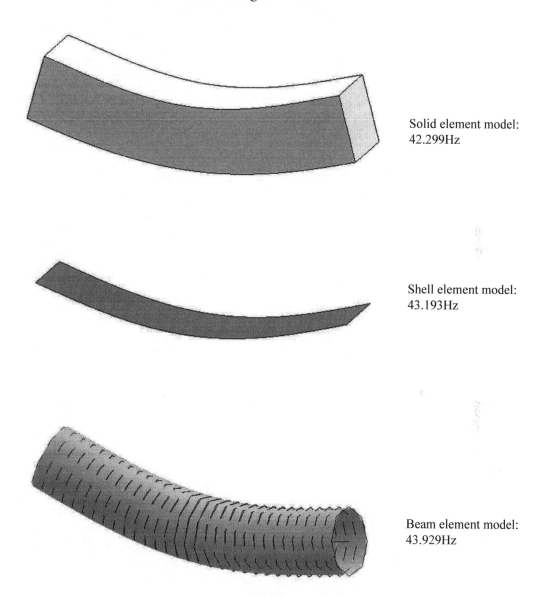

Solid element model: 42.299Hz

Shell element model: 43.193Hz

Beam element model: 43.929Hz

Figure 19-15: First mode of vibration of the solid, shell, and beam models.

All shapes correspond to the same first mode of vibration which is an in-plane mode. Colors are not available in modal plots in a Harmonic study.

All results closely match the exact solution of 42.710Hz.

NAFEMS TEST 5H

Deep Simply-Supported Beam; Harmonic Forced Vibration Response.

Figure 19-16: NAFEMS TEST 5H.

Geometry and material properties are the same as in NAFEMS TEST 5.

This test uses the same **SOLIDWORKS** model as NAFEMS TEST 5. The model is subjected to harmonic excitation by a uniformly distributed force:

$$F = 10^6 * sin\omega t \quad \text{where } \omega = 2\Pi f \quad 0 < f < 60 Hz$$

The frequency of excitation changes from 0 to 60Hz.

Modal Damping is 2% in all 16 modes to be used for analysis. **Rayleigh Damping may** be used alternatively to **Modal Damping**; the constants are α =5.36, β =7.46*10⁻⁵.

The test target is the peak displacement in the mid-span of 13.45mm, and the peak stress is 241.9MPa for the excitation frequency of 42.65Hz.

We'll expand the already defined studies for *TEST 5 solids, TEST 5 shells and TEST 5 beams* to obtain frequency response results.

Review the **Sensors** in each model configuration and define a load as shown in Figure 19-17. Define a **Modal Damping** of 2% for all modes.

Figure 19-17: Load to be used in the Frequency Response study.

Considering the load specified is 100000N/m and the beam length is 10m, the total load is 10000000N.

The illustration shows the surface model. Apply the same load to solid and beam models.

Define study properties as shown in Figure 19-18.

Frequency Options:
16 modes

Harmonic Options:
The range of excitation frequencies 0-60Hz

Advanced Options:
60 points for each frequency

Figure 19-18: Properties of Harmonic studies *TEST 5 solids*, *TEST 5 shells*, and *TEST 5 beams*.

16 modes are specified in the Frequency Options to satisfy the NAFEMS TEST 5H requirements. The appearance of windows has been modified to better fit this page.

Obtain the solutions and notice that there is only one modal frequency present in the specified range of frequencies 0-60Hz (Figure 19-19).

	Frequency (Hertz)		
Mode #	Solids	Shells	Beams
1	42.3	43.2	43.9
2	143.4	152.8	68.3
3	156.6	177.1	77.5
4	266.1	251.3	161.4
5	342.2	294.6	202.4
6	389.4	350.0	232.3
7	435.2	446.9	249.9
8	476.0	488.0	323.2
9	503.7	515.9	375.2
10	524.1	601.2	386.5
11	544.3	607.1	499.1
12	598.1	646.4	505.4
13	603.2	664.8	539.6
14	617.5	672.8	564.1
15	633.6	699.0	691.3
16	634.0	754.4	694.0

Figure 19-19: Modal frequency results of the three studies: *TEST 5 solids*, *TEST 5 shells* and *TEST 5 beams*.

In all studies there is only one mode in the range of 0-60Hz.

Observe that all solutions complete in 121 steps. This is because we specified 60 points for each frequency in the **Advanced Options** of the study properties. Considering that there is only one frequency in the range of 0-60Hz, there are 60 points on each side of the natural frequency plus one point for t = 0.

Review the sensor locations for all configurations and construct response graphs of the UY displacement component for all studies. All graphs report very close to the results of the NAFEMS TEST 5H benchmark results: 13.45mm at a frequency of excitation of 42.65Hz. A sample graph with results of the shell element model is shown in Figure 19-20.

Figure 19-20: UY displacement in the mid-span of the beam as a function of the excitation frequency.

In all studies there is only one mode in the range of 0-60Hz.

Another response graph could be constructed to see how close the stress results are to the NAFEMS TEST 5H stress target of 241.9MPa. Rather than constructing a response graph we review the stress plot for frequency step 61.

NAFEMS TEST 5H does not specify what stress component should be compared to the target value. Since the state of stress is predominantly bending, we'll look at the maximum bending stress component, which is the SX stress component. Notice that the SX stress reported is the same on the bottom and top of the shell elements. This is a **Frequency Response**, not a **Time Response** analysis, and in a **Frequency Response,** the maximum responses for a given excitation frequency are reported.

Follow Figure 19-21 to construct a plot of SX stress at frequency step 61.

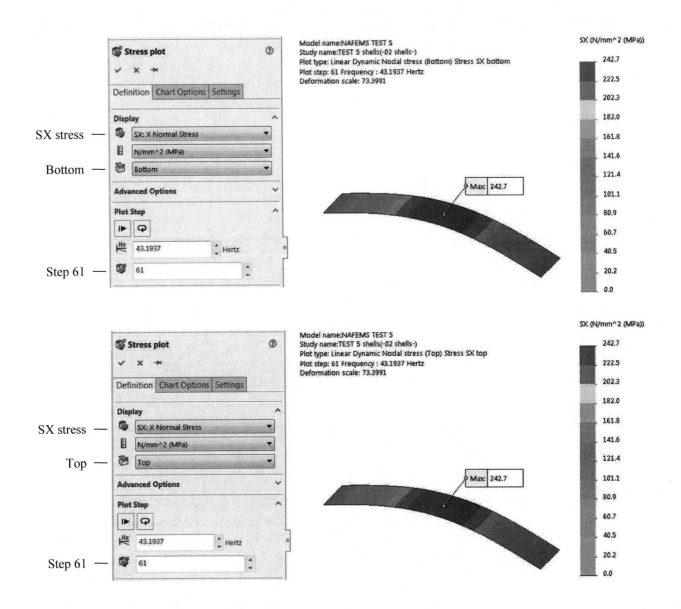

Figure 19-21: The SX stress component on the bottom and top of the shell elements at frequency step 61.

Step 61 corresponds to the natural frequency of 43.19Hz. Both plots show the same SX stress results.

NAFEMS TEST 5H specifies an alternative method of defining damping: **Rayleigh Damping** rather than **Modal Damping**. Repeat any of the completed studies with damping defined as **Rayleigh Damping** as shown in Figure 19-22. Don't forget to delete the **Modal Damping** that has been defined.

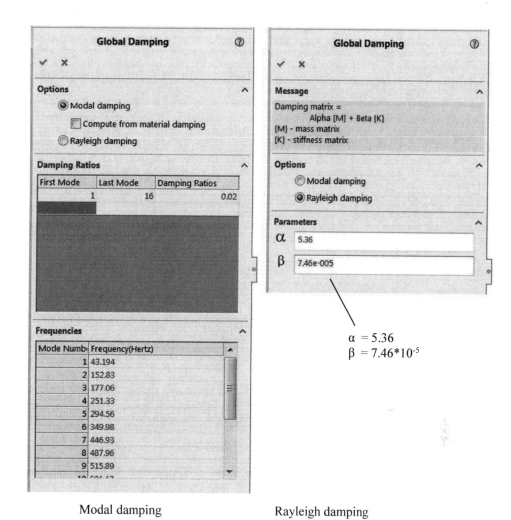

Modal damping   Rayleigh damping

Figure 19-22: Damping defined as Modal Damping and as Rayleigh damping.

Rayleigh damping coefficients are α =5.36, β =7.46*10⁻⁵ as specified in the NAFEMS TEST 5H benchmark test.

Obtain the solution with **Rayleigh Damping** to see that results are identical to those using **Modal Damping**.

NAFEMS TEST 5T

Deep Simply-Supported Beam; Transient Forced Vibration Response.

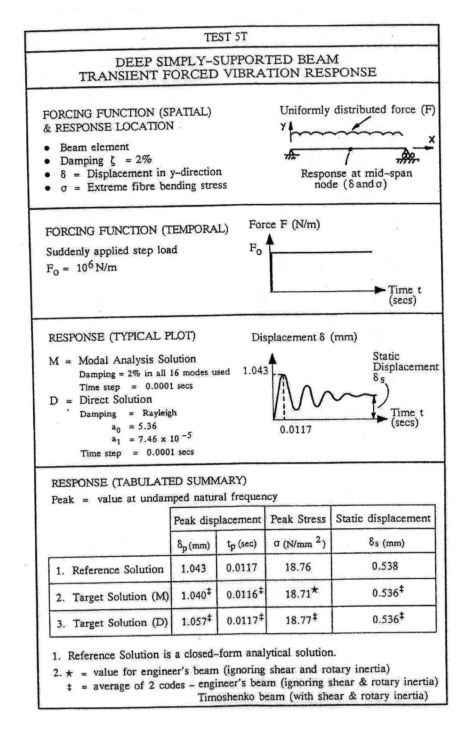

Figure 19-23: NAFEMS TEST 5T.

The model and material properties are the same as in NAFEMS TEST 5.

We'll stay with the same model NAFEMS TEST 5; benchmark test NAFEMS TEST 5T will be conducted with a **Modal Time History** study titled *TEST 5T* in only one configuration: *03 beams*. The model is subjected to a suddenly applied load $F_0 = 10^6 N/m$ as shown in Figure 19-24.

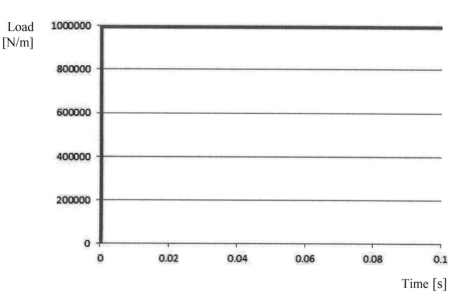

Figure 19-24: The load time history in NAFEMS TEST 5T.

Within the first 0.0001s the load increases to 100000N/m, then remains at this value for the rest of the analysis.

The **Time Step** to be used is 0.0001s; the **Modal Damping** is 2% in all 16 modes to be used for analysis. **Rayleigh Damping**, to be used alternatively to **Modal Damping**, is α =5.36, β =7.46*10^{-5}.

The test target is the displacement UY = 1.043mm in the mid-span of beam at time t = 0.0117s and static displacement ρ = 0.538mm (Figure 19-25).

Figure 19-25: Targets in NAFEMS TEST 5T.

Positive displacement is measured in the direction of the load.

The model NAFEMS TEST 5 already has three studies from the previous benchmark test NAFEMS TEST 5H. These studies are *TEST 5 solids, TEST 5 shells,* and *TEST 5 beams*. Move to the *03 beams* configuration and create a **Modal Time History** study titled *TEST 5T*. Instruct **Simulation** to treat the two solid bodies as beams and define restraints identical to those in study *TEST 5 beams*. Go through the **Edit Joints** dialog to recalculate the joints, and apply the load as shown in Figure 19-26.

(1)
Select both beams

(2)
Select Per unit length

(3)
Enter 1000000N/m

(4)
Select Curve

(5)
Define shock load as shown in the table

Figure 19-26: Load definition in the *Test 5T* study.

The load is uniformly distributed over two beams. Considering the length of 10m, the total load is $10^7 N$. Model is shown in wireframe display to show load which is applied to the center line corresponding to beam elements location.

Define the **Modal Time History** study properties as shown in Figure 19-27.

Figure 19-27: Properties of the Modal Time History (Time Response) study *TEST 5T.*

16 modes will be considered in the Modal Time History conducted in 1000 steps.

With time duration of 0.1s and a time step of 0.0001s, the analysis will complete in 1000 steps. This is the maximum number of steps allowed in a **Response Graph**.

Define a **Modal Damping** of 2% and run the solution. Construct the UY displacement **Response Graph** as shown in Figure 19-28.

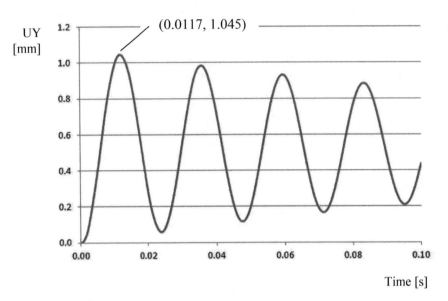

Figure 19-28: Time history of UY displacement in the mid-span of the beam during the first 0.1s.

The UY displacement at t = 0.0117s is 1.045mm, which closely matches the result of the NAFEMS TEST 5T.

Review the UY displacement time history and notice that the beam performs free damped vibration. After 0.0001s the shock load becomes a static load that causes static displacement once vibration stops. To see the static vibration we need to run the study for much longer than 0.1s.

Copy study *TEST 5T* into *TEST 5T 1s* and modify the study properties to make the total time 1s with a time step of 0.001s. This will again produce 1000 steps. The UY displacement time history during 1s is shown in Figure 19-29.

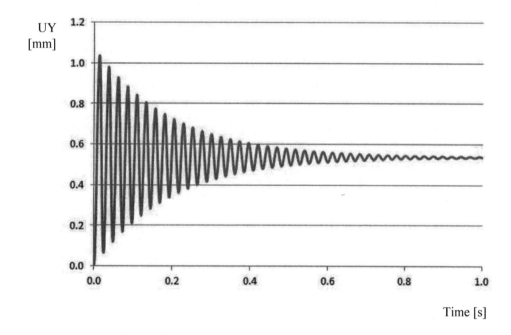

Figure 19-29: Time history of UY displacement in the mid-span of the beam during 1s.

Once the shock load ends, the beam performs free, damped vibration.

NAFEMS TEST 13

Simply-Supported Thin Square Plate.

TEST 13
SIMPLY-SUPPORTED THIN SQUARE PLATE

GEOMETRY & MESH

H.O.E. :   4 x 4 (as shown)

L.O.E. :   8 x 8

t = 0.05 m

ATTRIBUTES: (a) Well established
(b) Repeated eigenvalues

BOUNDARY CONDITIONS: $x = y = Rz$ at all nodes, $z = 0$ along all 4 edges

$Rx = 0$ along edges $x = 0$ & $x = 10m$, $Ry = 0$ along edges $y = 0$ & $y = 10m$

MATERIAL PROPERTIES: $E = 200 \times 10^9$ N/m^2 , $\nu = 0.3$, $\rho = 8000$ kg/m^3

ELEMENT TYPES: H.O.E.:   8–noded semi-loof thin shell element
L.O.E.:   4–noded iso-parametric shell element

FREQUENCIES & MODE SHAPES   (* = closed form solution)

$f_r^* = 2.377$ Hz
$f_t = 2.378$ Hz [HOE]
$= 2.418$ Hz [LOE]

Mode 1

$f_r^* = 5.942$ Hz
$f_t = 5.907$ Hz [HOE]
$= 6.332$ Hz [LOE]

Modes 2 & 3

$f_r^* = 9.507$ Hz
$f_t = 9.588$ Hz [HOE]
$= 10.192$ Hz [LOE]

Mode 4

$f_r^* = 11.884$ Hz
$f_t = 11.699$ Hz [HOE]
$= 13.991$ Hz [LOE]

Modes 5 & 6

$f_r^* = 15.449$ Hz
$f_t = 15.416$ Hz [HOE]
$= 17.748$ Hz [LOE]

Modes 7 & 8

Figure 19-30: NAFEMS TEST 13.

Carefully review the boundary conditions.

Open part model NAFEMS TEST 13 and notice a reference point in the center; it is there to locate a sensor. Materials properties require a custom material – the same as the one used in the previous tests.

Create a **Frequency** study titled *TEST 13*; specify eight modes in the study properties.

Define restraints to all four edges in the direction normal to the plate (Figure 19-31).

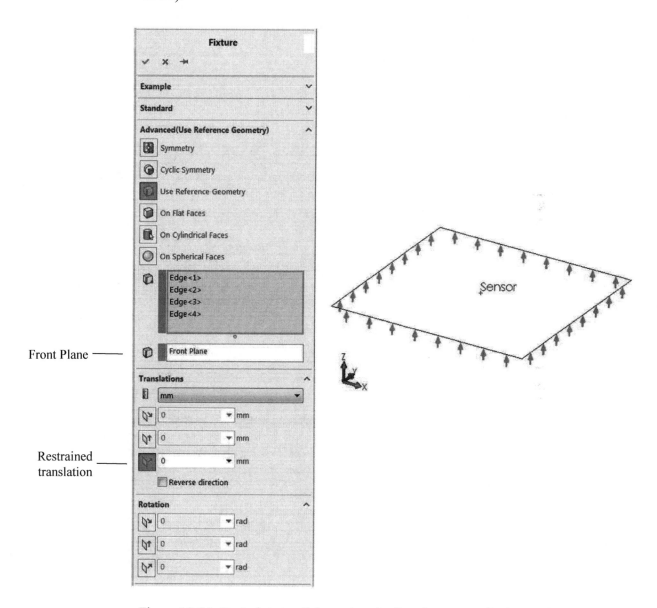

Front Plane

Restrained translation

Figure 19-31: Restraints to all four edges in direction perpendicular to plate.

The Front Plane is used as reference geometry.

Reference point called Sensor is placed in the center of face; it will be used to locate Workflow Sensitive Sensor.

Define restraints to the two edges parallel to the X axis as shown in Figure 19-32.

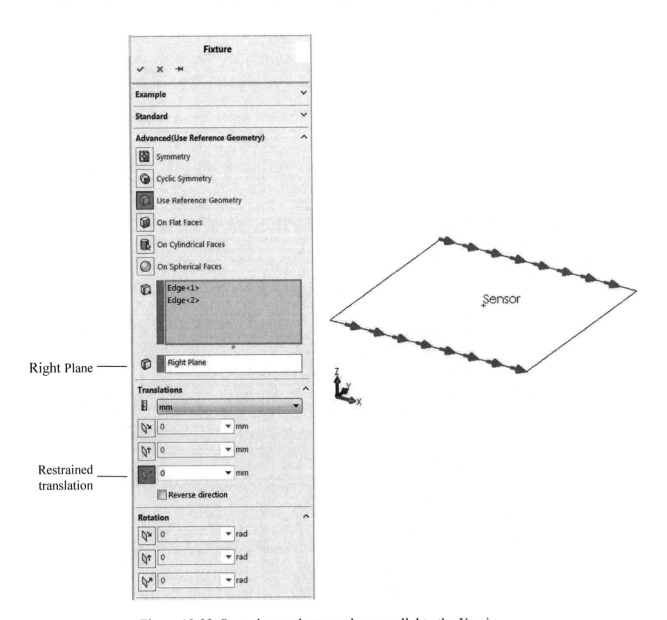

Figure 19-32: Restraints to the two edges parallel to the X axis.

The Right Plane is used as reference geometry.

Define restraints to the two edges parallel to the Y axis as shown in Figure 19-33.

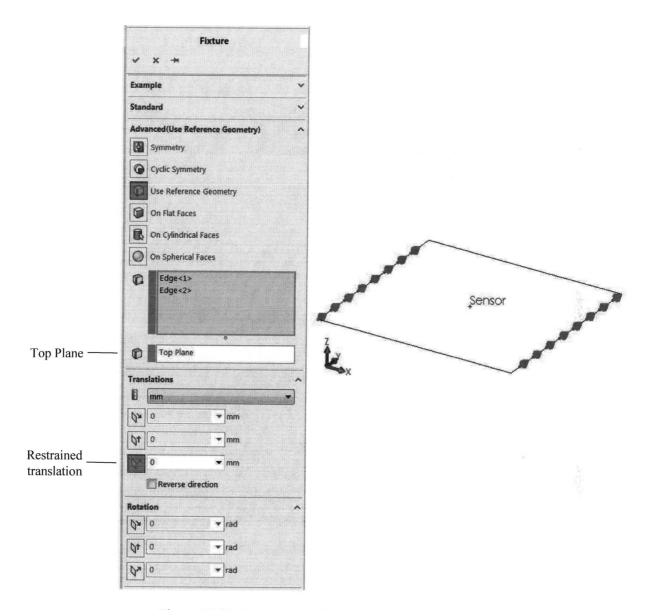

Top Plane

Restrained translation

Figure 19-33: Restraints to the two edges parallel to the Y axis.

The Top Plane is used as reference geometry.

Restraints shown in Figures 19-31, 19-32, and 19-33 fully restrain the model. There is no need to apply x = y = Rz = 0 at all nodes as specified in the test.

Define the shell thickness as 50mm and mesh the model with the default element size.

The first two modes of vibration are shown in Figure 19-34.

Mode 1: 2.374Hz

Mode 2: 5.926Hz

Figure 19-34: The first two modes of vibration and their frequencies.

Mode 1 is symmetric, mode 2 is anti-symmetric. Section Clipping is used to show the modal shapes more clearly.

The results of the modal analysis closely match the targets of NAFEMS TEST 13: 2.377Hz in the first mode and 5.942Hz in the second mode.

NAFEMS TEST 13R

Simply-Supported Thin Square Plate, Random Forced Vibration Response.
This study uses the NAFEMS TEST 13 model.

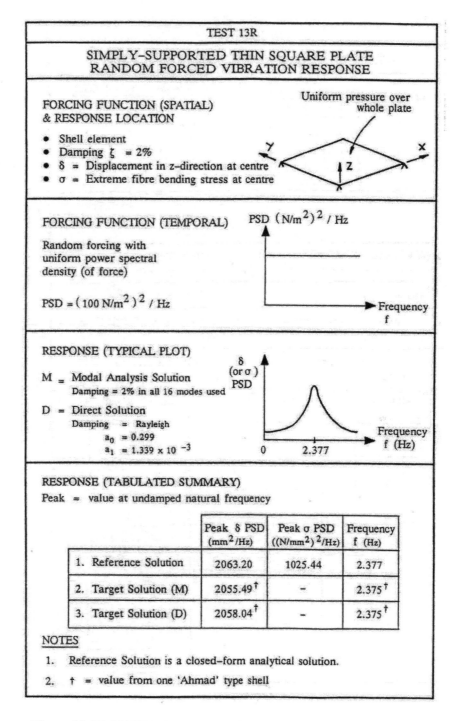

Figure 19-35: NAFEMS TEST 13R.

The model geometry and restraints are identical to study TEST 13.

Create a **Random** study titled *TEST 13R* and copy all restraints from the *TEST 13* study.

The load is a random force with uniform Power Spectral Density which is a white noise.

The force is a pressure; $p = (100N/m^2)^2/Hz$. Define the load as shown in Figure 19-36. Remember that the pressure must be entered in units of $(N/m^2)^2/Hz$. Therefore, its numerical value is $p = (100N/m^2)^2/Hz = 100^2$ $(N/m^2)^2/Hz = 10000 (N/m^2)^2/Hz$. The use of incorrect units is a common source of error in random vibration analyses.

Figure 19-36: NAFEMS TEST 13R.

The frequency curve window defines a uniform PSD curve in the frequency range of 0-100Hz. Notice what the units of pressure are.

Define a **Modal Damping** of 2% for 16 modes in **Global Damping** definition window.

Define a **Random** study with properties as shown in Figure 19-37.

Figure 19-37: Properties of study *TEST 13R*.

40 frequency points are specified in the Random Vibration Options to have smooth graphs.

Define the **Result Options** using the Sensor in the center of plate and obtain the solution.

Construct a **Response Graph** of the PSD displacement (Figure 19-38).

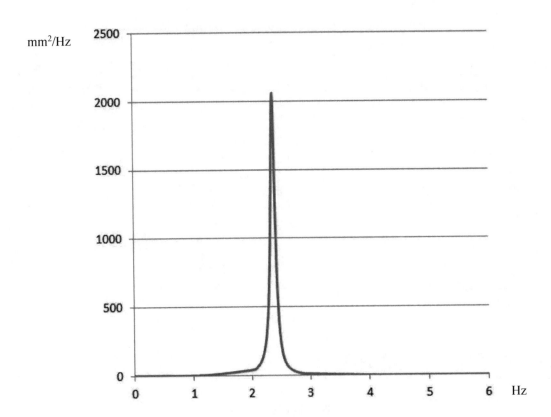

Figure 19-38: The PSD displacement response graph.

The first mode dominates the vibration response in the frequency range of 0-6Hz.

Review the graph and notice that the maximum PSD displacement closely matches the NAFEMS TEST 13R result of 2063mm²/Hz.

To complete the analysis of the Random Vibration problem, review RMS displacements plot shown in Figure 19-39.

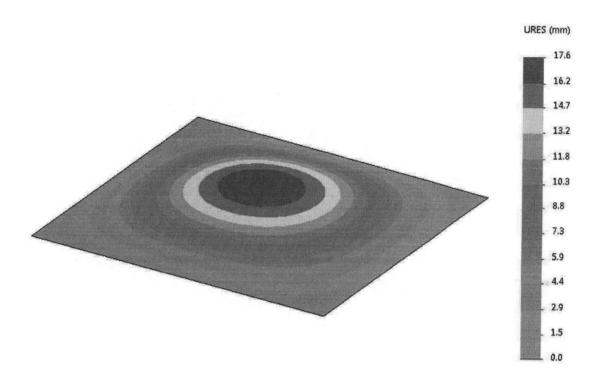

Figure 19-39: RMS value of displacement.

One value of the RMS displacements is reported for the whole range of excitation 0-6Hz.

20: Glossary of terms

Critical Damping

System damping above which oscillations are not possible.

Degrees of Freedom

Independent variables describing position (linear or angular) of a rigid body or of a node in a finite element mesh.

Discrete Vibrating System

System components responsible for inertial, damping and elastic properties are separated. It takes the form of an assembly of rigid bodies connected by springs and dampers.

Distributed Vibrating System

System components responsible for inertial, damping and elastic properties are not separated. It takes the form of an assembly of elastic bodies.

Dynamic Analysis

Analysis of motion of rigid bodies and flexible bodies.

Flexible body

Body that deforms under applied loads. Flexible body must have elastic properties defined.

Frequency Analysis

SOLIDWORKS Simulation term used to denote Modal Analysis.

Frequency Response Analysis

Analysis of vibration caused by loads defined as function of frequency rather than of time.

Impulse load

Load of a short duration defined as a function of time.

Harmonic Analysis

SOLIDWORKS Simulation term used to denote Frequency Response Analysis.

Kinematic Pair

Connection between two bodies that imposes constraints on relative movements of the bodies.

Linear Damping

Damping in linear motion.

Mechanism

System of rigid and/or elastic bodies connected by kinematic pairs, working together in a machine.

Modal Analysis

Finding modes of vibration of a vibrating system.

Modal Damping

% of critical damping present in a Single Degree of Freedom System.

Modal Superposition Method

Method that represents a vibrating system as a collection of Single Degree of Freedom Oscillators (SDOF); each SDOF represents the system vibrating in a given mode of vibration. The vibration response of the system is found as a superposition of vibration responses of those individual SDOFs.

Mode of Vibration

Certain combination of frequency and shape of vibration for which cancellation between inertial and elastic effects takes place.

Modal Time History

SOLIDWORKS Simulation term used to denote Time Response Analysis.

Random Vibration Analysis

Analysis of vibration due to stationary, random excitation given in the form of the Power Spectral Density.

Rayleigh Damping

Damping used in nonlinear vibration analysis; damping matrix is expressed as a linear combination of mass and stiffness matrices.

Response Spectrum Analysis

Type of vibration analysis used to analyze vibration caused by non-stationary excitation such as a seismic shock.

Rigid Body Mode

Mode of vibration of a structure without support or with a partial support. Program assigns 0Hz frequency to modes corresponding to rigid body displacements.

Rigid Body Motion

Translation and/or rotation of a body without deformation.

Single Degree of Freedom Oscillator

A mass (rigid body) connected to a base with a spring (and sometimes damper). It performs linear or angular oscillations and its motions are fully described by one unknown.

Structure

An elastic body capable of supporting loads. Structure is fully supported and it can't move without deforming. Movement of structure takes form of oscillations about the position of equilibrium.

Time Response Analysis

Analysis of vibration caused by loads defined as function time.

Vibration Analysis

Analysis of motion of a deformable (elastic) body or system about an equilibrium point.

Viscous Damping

Damping force is proportional to velocity.

21: References

This textbook builds on an understanding of structural analysis with the Finite Element Method and assumes familiarity with structural and introductory modal analysis to the extent covered in the introductory textbook: Kurowski P. "Engineering Analysis with SOLIDWORKS Simulation," SDC Publications.

For a review of the topics discussed in this book, readers are referred to the following literature listed here in the order of relevance:

1. Kurowski P. "Engineering Analysis with SOLIDWORKS Simulation 2016"

2. Inman D., "Engineering Vibration" Prentice Hall

3. The Standard NAFEMS Benchmarks, NAFEMS

4. Selected Benchmarks for Forced Vibration, NAFEMS

5. How to Do Seismic Analysis Using Finite Elements NAFEMS

6. How to undertake Finite Element Based Vibration Analysis NAFEMS

7. Vibrationdata.com

8. Logan D. "A First Course in the Finite Element Method," Brooks/Cole

9. Adams V., Askenazi A. "Building Better Products with Finite Element Analysis," OnWord Press

10. Kim N.H., Sankar B.V. "Introduction to Finite Element Analysis and Design," John Wiley & Sons, Inc.

The full list of NAFEMS publications can be found at www.nafems.org. Another internet site with a number of FEA related publications is presented by Design Generator Inc. at www.designgenerator.com/publications.htm.

22: List of exercises

Chapter	Part	Assembly	Spreadsheets Animations Text files
Cover page	2016 COVER PAGE*		
1	TRUSS CLIP*	ELLIPTIC TRAMMEL** HELICOPTER PLANAR PRISMATIC REVOLUTE CYLINDRICAL SPHERICAL SCREW DISCRETE LINEAR* SWING ARM* DOUBLE PENDULUM WRECKING BALL**	
2	BALL VALVE PLATE		
3	NOTCH		
4	ROTOR COLUMN	COLUMN***	
5	U BRACKET		
6	BEAM DEMO*	SHAFT	
7	CAR		
8	VASE		
9	BAJA FRAME		
10	FLAT*	PLIERS*	

11		MDOF	MDOF.xlsx MDOF IMPULSE.xlsx
12	ELBOW PIPE	SHAKER TABLE***	
13		CENTRIFUGE	CENTRIFUGE.xlsx
14	SUPPORT		
15		VIB ABSORBER	
16		HD HEAD	HD HEAD.xlsx
17		FRAME	FRAME.xlsx
18	PLANK		PLANK.xlsx PLANK RAYLEIGH.xlsx
19	NAFEMS TEST FV2 NAFEMS TEST 5 NAFEMS TEST 13		

*   Includes Simulation study ready to run
**   Includes Motion study ready to animate
***   For illustration only